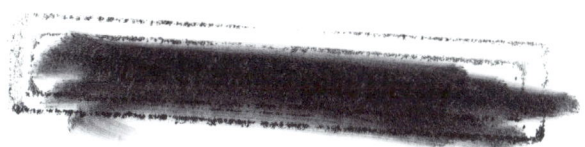

D-DAY:
THE NORMANDY INVASION

D-DAY:
THE NORMANDY INVASION

BY MARCIA AMIDON LUSTED

CONTENT CONSULTANT
PETER R. MANSOOR, PHD
GENERAL RAYMOND E. MASON JR.
CHAIR IN MILITARY HISTORY
OHIO STATE UNIVERSITY

CREDITS

Published by ABDO Publishing Company, PO Box 398166, Minneapolis, MN 55439. Copyright © 2014 by Abdo Consulting Group, Inc. International copyrights reserved in all countries. No part of this book may be reproduced in any form without written permission from the publisher. The Essential Library™ is a trademark and logo of ABDO Publishing Company.

Printed in the United States of America,
North Mankato, Minnesota
102013
012014

 THIS BOOK CONTAINS AT LEAST 10% RECYCLED MATERIALS.

Editor: Rebecca Rowell
Series Designer: Becky Daum

Photo credits: US Coast Guard, cover, 2, 88; Bettmann/Corbis, 6, 36; AP Images, 13, 14, 19, 39, 41, 59, 69, 70, 73; Corbis, 26, 34, 55, 60, 80; Red Line Editorial, 28; US Army, 42, 63, 78; SHAEF, 49; Charles E. Steinheimer/Time & Life Pictures/Getty Images, 50; The Mariners' Museum/Corbis, 76; Three Lions/Hulton Archive/Getty Images, 87; iStockphoto/Thinkstock, 95

Library of Congress Control Number: 2013946964

Cataloging-in-Publication Data

Lusted, Marcia Amidon, 1962-
 D-Day: the Normandy invasion / Marcia Amidon Lusted.
   p. cm. -- (Essential events)
Includes bibliographical references and index.
ISBN 978-1-62403-259-2
1. World War, 1939-1945--Campaigns--France--Normandy--Juvenile literature. 2. Normandy (France)--History--Juvenile literature.   I. Title.
940.54--dc23

2013946964

CONTENTS

CHAPTER 1
TAKING A GAMBLE 6

CHAPTER 2
GETTING INVOLVED 14

CHAPTER 3
PLANNING AND PREPARING 28

CHAPTER 4
DECEIVING THE ENEMY 42

CHAPTER 5
GEARING UP 50

CHAPTER 6
LOADING AND LAUNCHING 60

CHAPTER 7
GOING ASHORE 70

CHAPTER 8
BEACH BY BEACH 78

CHAPTER 9
THE NEXT DAY AND BEYOND 88

Timeline   96
Essential Facts   100
Glossary   102
Additional Resources   104
Source Notes   106
Index   110
About the Author   112
About the Consultant   112

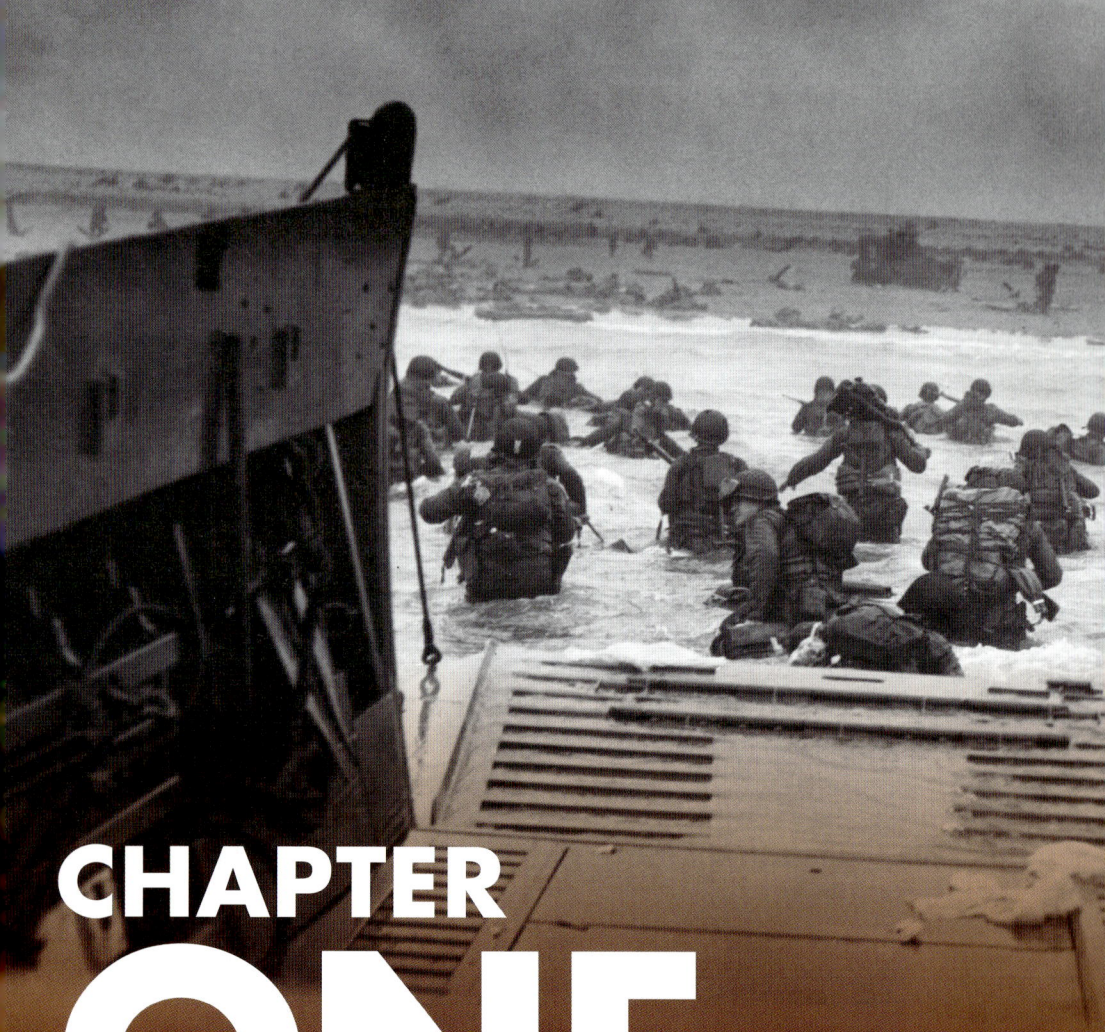

CHAPTER ONE

TAKING A GAMBLE

It was just after dawn on June 6, 1944. The beaches of Normandy, on the northwest coast of France, were alive with activity. The commotion was not caused by locals enjoying the shoreline or the cool waters of the English Channel. Far from it.

The largest amphibious military operation in history was under way. It was World War II (1939–1945), and the continent was under the brutal occupation of the German Nazis. Germany controlled Europe as Adolf Hitler and his Nazi forces invaded its nations one by one, occupying France in 1940. But the United Kingdom, the Soviet Union, the United States, and their allies—the Allied powers—refused to give in to Germany and its allies, the Axis powers. On this cold June morning, the invading Allied forces included men from 12 countries. Most of the troops were from Canada, the United Kingdom, and the United States. Australia, Belgium, Czechoslovakia, France, Greece, the Netherlands, New Zealand, Norway, and Poland also sent men to fight.

US troops head toward Normandy's shore to battle German soldiers on June 6, 1944.

Allied fighters and bombers had destroyed much of the Luftwaffe, Germany's air force. They had also interrupted transportation throughout France by bombing rail lines and bridges. More than 23,000 Allied paratroopers had dropped behind enemy lines into France to seize critical terrain and protect the beaches from German counterattacks.[1]

At the same time, 125,000 Allied troops approached the region's five beaches—code-named Sword, Juno,

THE AXIS AND ALLIED POWERS

The nations that fought in World War II did so as part of the Axis or Allied powers. The Axis powers were Germany, Italy, and Japan, supported by several minor allies. These three countries agreed Germany was in control of most of Europe, Italy controlled the Mediterranean, and Japan controlled East Asia and the Pacific. They had in common the desire to gain territory through military conquest, overthrow the balance of power established after World War I (1914–1918), and destroy Soviet Communism.

The Allied powers were the United Kingdom, the United States, the Soviet Union, and China, as well as France when it was not under German occupation. In addition, all the wartime members of the newly founded and still provisional United Nations were considered part of the Allied powers. This added several nations to the Allied ranks, including Australia, Belgium, Canada, Costa Rica, Cuba, Czechoslovakia, the Dominican Republic, Greece, Guatemala, Haiti, Honduras, India, Luxembourg, the Netherlands, New Zealand, Nicaragua, Norway, Panama, Poland, El Salvador, South Africa, and Yugoslavia. Six additional Allies joined during the war: the Philippines, Mexico, Ethiopia, Iraq, Free French, and Free Danes. These nations were united by the goal of stopping Germany and its allies.

Gold, Omaha, and Utah—in ships, landing craft, and amphibious tanks.[2] The booming of huge guns filled the air as Allied battleships, cruisers, and destroyers tried to clear a path on shore for these forces. Gunners shot over soldiers' heads into the heavily fortified German emplacements. Antitank obstacles, underwater mines, barbed wire, and still more mines further guarded the beaches. The Germans had been awaiting invasion for years and were ready for such an attack.

Getting to Shore

The initial moments of trying to get out of the water and onto land were not easy. The first wave of troops who approached Normandy's shore rode in small landing craft called Higgins boats. The front of these vessels had ramps that could be dropped to allow soldiers to exit directly onto the beach. But getting on the beaches turned out to be much more difficult than imagined.

Malvin Pike, a sergeant in E Company of the Second Battalion, Eighth Infantry, Fourth Division of the US Army, exited his boat before reaching its destination. The ramp got stuck approaching Utah Beach:

> I jumped out in waist-deep water. We had 200 feet [61 m] to go to shore and you couldn't run, you could

just kind of push forward. We finally made it to the edge of the water, then we had 200 yards [183 m] of open beach to cross, through the obstacles.[3]

The challenges were far more harrowing than soldiers simply getting off their boats. Many Allied troops were killed before they reached the beach. Alfred Sears, an electrician's mate in the US Army's 116th Regiment, described landing on Omaha Beach:

We hit the sandbar, dropped the ramp, and then all hell poured loose on us. The soldiers in the boat received a hail of machine-gun bullets. The Army Lieutenant was immediately killed, shot through the head.[4]

Some troops were forced into the water and tried to swim. This was a difficult task because the men were loaded down with weapons and

---

D-DAY ON SCREEN

Many films focus on D-day. *The Longest Day* (1962), starring John Wayne, presents the story from both sides: Allied and German. Steven Spielberg directed *Saving Private Ryan* (1998), for which he won an Academy Award. The film begins with an extended scene of the landing on Omaha Beach on D-day from the viewpoint of a Ranger captain taking part. The movie was praised for its realistic portrayal of war. A few years later, cable network HBO presented the ten-part miniseries *Band of Brothers* (2001). The program follows a single company of the US Army from D-day through August 15, 1945, when Japan surrendered.

equipment. Many drowned. Those who made it ashore were met by heavy defensive gunfire. Several were clustered in groups, which made them easy targets for the Germans.

Some troops were killed as they pushed forward with the operation, moving off the beaches and inland. Coming ashore was only one piece of an elaborate plan intended to defeat Germany.

Sunset at Normandy

By the end of the day, casualties numbered between 14,000 and 19,000.[5] This included Allied and German servicemen, as well as French civilians. The invasion of Normandy, named Operation Overlord, was a gamble for the Allied forces. But military strategists believed it was a necessary risk. Without it, the war would be prolonged, and Germany's Nazi Party would maintain its reign of power over continental Europe.

HITLER'S INITIAL OPTIMISM

When news reached Hitler of the Allied landings in Normandy, he was optimistic at first. He told the chief of his headquarters, Field Marshal Wilhelm Keitel, "The news couldn't be better. As long as they were in Britain, we couldn't get at them. Now, we have them where we can destroy them."[6]

THE MEANING OF D-DAY

Over the years, many people have wondered what the *D* in D-day stands for. Speculations include *decision*, *disembarkation*, and *departed*. It is a military term started by the US Army during World War I and stands for the day of an operation: *D* for day. H-hour is the time of an operation. D-day would be used because the date was not yet known or needed to be kept secret. The term has variations. D–1 is the day before an operation, while D+1 is the day after an operation. D-day has been used for many operations, but since June 6, 1944, it has come to refer especially to that specific date.

The Normandy invasion was the result of careful planning and preparation by political and military leaders of multiple nations. The result was an operation that required Allies to put everything on the line with an all-out attack on German forces. This one day, D-day, would help turn the tide of World War II in Europe and help the Allies defeat Hitler and Germany's armed forces, the Wehrmacht.

Wounded US troops who stormed the beaches of Normandy take a break for food.

CHAPTER TWO

GETTING INVOLVED

The road that led to the events of D-day started with a war more than two decades earlier: World War I. This first and terrible world war raged in Europe from 1914 to 1918. The United States did not want to get involved in what it perceived as a European war. However, in 1917, President Woodrow Wilson felt the United States no longer had a choice. German U-boats, or submarines, were preying on merchant ships in the Atlantic Ocean. And Germany proposed to Mexico to attack the American Southwest.

When the war ended on November 11, 1918, issues with Germany remained. Primarily, they involved the place of a rising Germany in the European balance of power. Still, it seemed the world would remain peaceful. The Treaty of Versailles forced Germany to pay large reparations for the war and blamed the entire conflict on the Germans. This led to severe resentment. A legend soon grew among the German people that their army had remained unbeaten at the end of the

Adolf Hitler led Europe into its second war in the 1900s.

FROM DEMOCRACY TO DICTATORSHIP

Following World War I, Germany had a new government. The Weimar Republic replaced the monarchy in 1919. The republic was Germany's attempt at a democratic government. Citizens elected its president and parliament, and there was a bill of rights. Eventually, Hitler rose to power and was selected chancellor of the republic in 1933. This marked the end of the republic. Once in power, Hitler created a dictatorship.

war but had been betrayed by Communists, Socialists, and Jews who supposedly incited the 1918 revolution that toppled the kaiser and his imperial government.

When the 1930s brought financial woes with the Great Depression, the democratically elected Weimar government in Germany collapsed. This led to Adolf Hitler and the Nazi Party's success in the election of 1933. Hitler had campaigned on a platform of extreme nationalism. He soon assumed dictatorial powers. He rejected the Versailles Treaty, rearmed Germany's armed forces, and led his nation on the path to another world war. It started with the *Anschluss*, or "union," in which Hitler's Nazis marched into Austria unopposed and took control of the country in 1938. Hitler followed with invasions of Czechoslovakia and Poland in 1939. On September 3, the United Kingdom, Australia, France, and New

Zealand declared war on Germany following its invasion of Poland two days before.

A Policy of Isolation

At the end of World War I, the United States retreated into isolationism. The US Congress failed to ratify the Versailles Treaty. So, the United States did not join the League of Nations, the multinational body that would supposedly ensure collective security and peace in the world.

To avoid becoming tangled in another global conflict in the future, Congress passed a series of Neutrality Acts in the 1930s. These laws prohibited the export of weapons, ammunition, and other war supplies from the United States to any country at war. They also banned US banks from making loans to nations at war. The laws did allow the United States to sell raw materials to warring countries, but only as long as the purchasers paid cash and the items were not transported on US ships.

Helping Its Allies

Hitler's legions made their way across continental Europe after the start of the war in 1939. They took

HITLER'S PLAN

Hitler wanted a German empire in which German-speaking peoples dominated the world. He wanted it to be racially pure, purged of any undesirable people. These included persons of Jewish origin, Gypsies, the mentally ill, the physically disabled, homosexuals, and anyone else he considered inferior and a threat to his idea of a pure German race.

Hitler and the Nazis' mass slaughtering of millions of people in Europe is known as the Holocaust. The Nazis killed approximately 6 million Jewish people, plus millions of others they deemed inferior or who were prisoners of war, political opponents, or religious dissenters.[1]

over more countries, including Denmark, Norway, France, Belgium, Luxembourg, and the Netherlands in 1940. The Nazis killed millions of people and imprisoned tens of millions. The United States' former allies from World War I, the United Kingdom and France, struggled greatly. They needed arms and supplies to counter the German war machine.

In December 1940, President Franklin D. Roosevelt decided to provide supplies and military goods to the United Kingdom. He convinced Congress to modify the Neutrality Acts and committed the US Navy to provide defense against German U-boats in the Atlantic.

By this time, Japan had joined forces with Germany and Italy—the Axis powers. And on December 7, 1941, Japan attacked the US naval base at Pearl Harbor,

German soldiers lead away Polish Jews in Warsaw, Poland, as the ghetto where they lived is destroyed.

Hawaii. Hitler did not know about the attack before it happened, but he was pleased by it, saying, "We can't lose the war at all. We now have an ally which has never been conquered in 3,000 years."[2]

The next day, Congress voted to declare war on Japan. Hitler, who was already in a war against the Soviet Union, followed suit by declaring war on the United States on December 11. Isolationism disappeared overnight as the United States joined the United Kingdom, the Soviet Union, and the other members of the Allied powers in a massive world war.

Germany First

The United States eventually engaged Axis forces in Europe, North Africa, mainland Asia, and the islands of the Pacific, as well as across the world's seas and skies. In Europe and North Africa, US troops would battle German and Italian forces. In the Pacific, they would fight against Japan.

Roosevelt and his military advisers decided on a strategy that has come to be known as "Germany First."[3] Because Germany posed the greatest military threat to the West and had a stronger military than Japan, the Allies would focus their resources on defeating Germany before turning their full power against Japan.

In practice, this strategy was hard to implement. The American people demanded revenge against the Japanese. US military commanders in the Pacific—General Douglas MacArthur and Admiral Chester Nimitz—demanded forces to defend Hawaii and protect the line of communication to Australia. And beginning in

> "No matter how long it may take us to overcome this premeditated invasion, the American people . . . will win through to absolute victory. I believe that I interpret the will of the Congress and of the people when I assert that we will not only defend ourselves to the uttermost but will make it very certain that this form of treachery shall never again endanger us. . . . With confidence in our armed forces, with the unbounding determination of our people, we will gain the inevitable triumph—so help us God."[4]
> —President Franklin D. Roosevelt, December 8, 1941, asking Congress to declare war on Japan

August 1942, the forces would be needed to launch a counteroffensive against Japanese forces on the island of Guadalcanal and in New Guinea.

Initially, the European theater greatly favored the Germans, who enjoyed many victories and conquered most of Europe in the process. The United Kingdom staved off defeat during the Battle of Britain in the fall of 1940 but could not beat the Germans alone. Hitler's invasion of the Soviet Union in June 1941 changed the situation greatly. After the Red Army defeated the German army outside Moscow in December, things began to change. The Wehrmacht made one last attempt to conquer the Soviet Union in 1942 but lost. The Red Army's victory in the Battle of Stalingrad dramatically altered the strategic momentum of the war.

Operation Torch

The Allies had trouble agreeing on a plan for defeating Hitler. General George C. Marshall, the US Army's chief of staff, thought the best plan was to use massive military force to confront Hitler head-on as early as 1942 and 1943. But the British were concerned the Allies were not ready for this kind of massive battle against Germany's superior military force. The British believed US forces had not yet organized themselves enough. As a newer participant in the war, the United States needed time to mobilize its forces.

The Soviet Union wanted the Western Allies to start a new front against Germany in Europe. British prime minister Winston Churchill preferred working to weaken Germany and Italy by attacking in the Mediterranean—and perhaps Norway—instead of confronting the Wehrmacht head-on in France.

German forces in North Africa under the skilled tactical leadership of Field Marshal Erwin Rommel had many successes. By summer 1942, they had moved deep into Egypt. But in October, British general Bernard Montgomery and the Eighth Army defeated Rommel's forces in the Battle of El Alamein.

In July 1942, Churchill had convinced Roosevelt to begin planning the invasion of the Vichy French possessions in northwest Africa as a start to further operations in Europe. There, the Allies would meet less resistance and immobilize German and Italian forces. The invasion plan called for amphibious landings on the Atlantic coast of Morocco and in the Mediterranean at Oran and Algiers, Algeria. The invasion, code-named Operation Torch, was especially important. It would be the first major commitment of US ground forces outside the Pacific. It would also be the first time British and US ground forces would fight together outside that theater. Until this time, the British had made up the bulk of Allied troops in North Africa and held overall command in that theater. In time, the British and the Americans would form a formidable team.

The attacks started before dawn on November 8. The Allied forces met resistance from French troops who were part of the Vichy government that controlled the southern part of France not occupied by German forces. Although the Allies met stiff resistance in places,

VICHY FRANCE

During World War II, France was a divided country in several ways. Early in the war, in 1940, France surrendered to Germany, which then occupied three-fifths of French territory. The government of the remainder of France was based in the city of Vichy and headed by Henri Philippe Pétain, a World War I general. This government is referred to as Vichy France. The Vichy government allowed the Germans to take French resources, sent French citizens to Germany as forced labor, and cooperated in the Nazi deportation of Jews to death camps in Poland. Although the Vichy government believed these measures might allow it to keep some control over the part of France not occupied by German forces, it was a false hope. Those who did not agree with the Vichy government joined the Free French and were supported by the United Kingdom. The Free French, led by Charles de Gaulle, helped to organize the resistance movement in occupied France and prepare the French people for the D-day invasion.

they achieved their objectives within two days. After the invasion succeeded, many of the French troops switched sides and later fought alongside the Allies as part of the Free French forces.

The Allies learned valuable lessons about amphibious assault from Operation Torch. For example, the beach at Oran had not been scouted thoroughly before the invasion. Allied forces sent more than 18,000 troops and a considerable amount of equipment to Oran.[6] The water proved to be too shallow. This damaged some

CALLED TO SERVE

The United States relied on a draft to obtain servicemen to fight in World War II. The nation had used conscription, or mandatory military service, during the American Civil War (1861–1865) and World War I. Initially, American men ages 25 to 40 were required to register for military service. If called upon by the government, they would actively serve. The government expanded the range to ages 18 to 45 for World War I.

In 1940, the Selective Training and Service Act became the first peacetime conscription. All male citizens between ages 21 and 36 were required to comply. However, it was the first time a man could be exempt from service by being a conscientious objector. At first, the draft called for one year of service. Once the nation entered World War II, the government changed the length to the duration of the war. Between November 1940 and October 1946, approximately 45 million men registered for the draft, and more than 10 million of them were called upon to serve.[5]

of the landing craft, which were weighed down with soldiers and gear.

Despite its flaws, Operation Torch boosted the morale of the Allied troops. The Allies now believed they could successfully plan and carry out a large amphibious attack while working together. The subsequent fighting in Tunisia exposed flaws in how the US Army was prepared for combat. But US military leaders and soldiers learned from this experience and emerged more effective.

The Allies invaded Sicily in July 1943. The operation led to Italy's withdrawal from the war and the removal of its dictator, Benito Mussolini, from power. The Allied invasion at Salerno in September established Allied forces in southern Italy. But stiff German resistance in the mountains south of Rome hindered the Allied advance north, up the Italian mainland.

The Directive

As operations in Italy progressed, Roosevelt, Churchill, and Soviet premier Joseph Stalin—known as the "Big Three"—met in Tehran, Iran, in November 1943 to coordinate an alliance strategy.[7] There, they agreed on an invasion of France to take place the next spring.

The Big Three were, *from left to right*, Winston Churchill, Franklin D. Roosevelt, and Joseph Stalin.

Following the conference, Roosevelt appointed General Dwight D. Eisenhower to the position of supreme allied commander for the forthcoming invasion. In that role, Eisenhower was made responsible for planning and executing the campaign in northwest Europe that would be necessary to defeat Hitler and Germany. If successful, it would change the course of the war.

The planning for this invasion had begun before Eisenhower's appointment, under the direction of Lieutenant General Sir Frederick Morgan of the United Kingdom. Morgan's staff completed a great deal of groundwork, including studying various landing sites and drafting an idea for the invasion.

The Allied victories in North Africa, Sicily, and Italy in 1942 and 1943 had proven US forces capable. These successes also showed the strength of the alliance between the United States and the United Kingdom. It was time to invade Hitler's *Festung Europa*, or "Fortress Europe," and prepare the Allied forces for the decisive campaign in northwest Europe that would help decide the outcome of World War II.

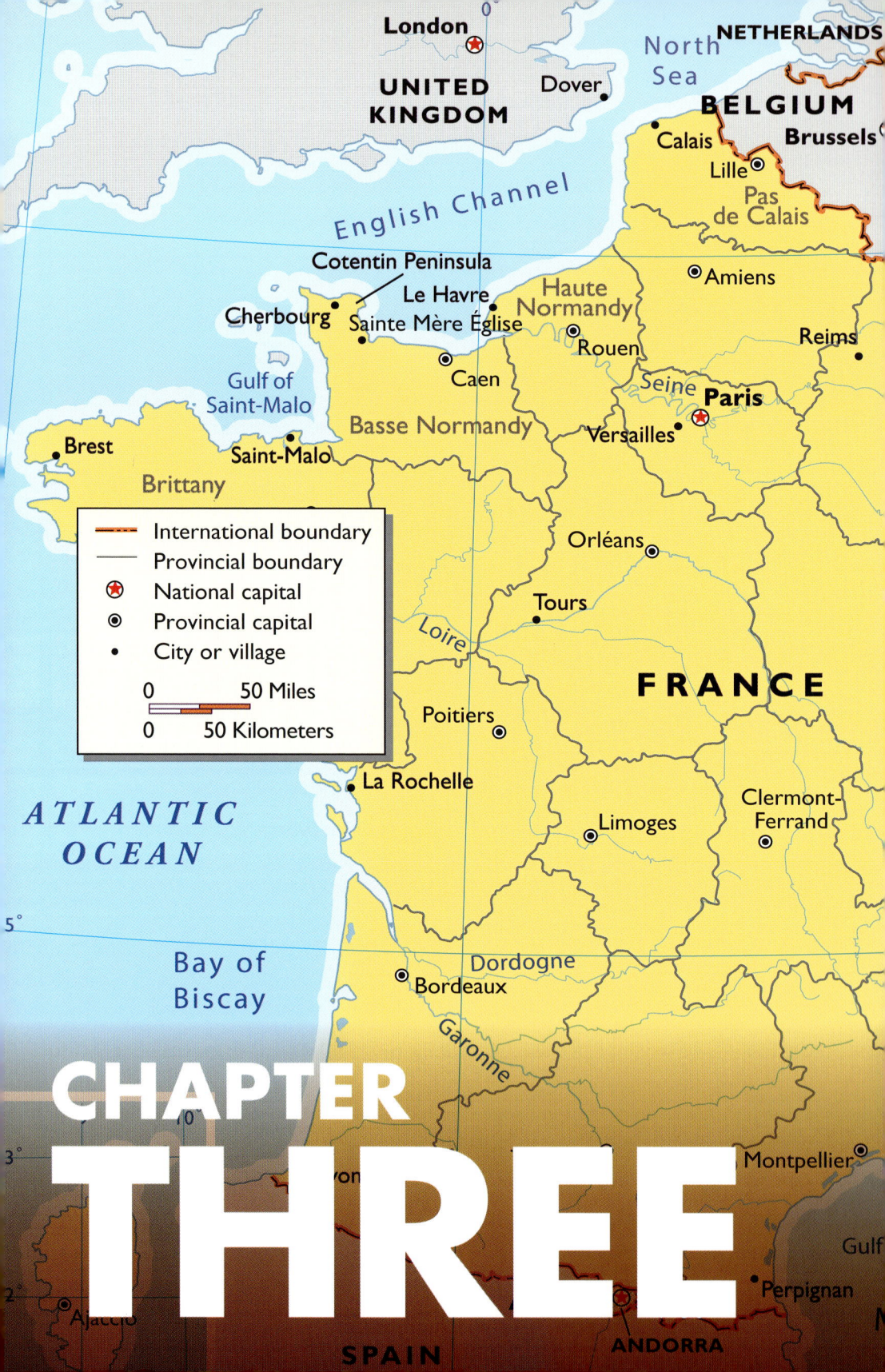

PLANNING AND PREPARING

By 1944, the Allied powers had decided on their attack route: the English Channel. That body of water is approximately 350 miles (563 km) long and ranges from 20 to 150 miles (32 to 241 km) wide. It separates the United Kingdom from France and the rest of the European continent. Crossing it to carry out an amphibious attack against Germany's stronghold in France would require careful planning. The last successful opposed military crossing had taken place nearly 900 years before. It was when William the Conqueror invaded England from Normandy—the opposite direction the Allies would travel in 1944.

Amphibious assaults were difficult. Few armies and navies had successfully carried them out. But the Allied forces' successful amphibious attacks in 1942 in North Africa and 1943 in Sicily showed that, with proper planning, such attacks were not impossible. Allied

Crossing the English Channel and launching a successful attack against German forces would require careful and thorough planning by the Allies.

leaders would examine the lessons learned from these invasions as they organized the invasion of France.

Planning Operation Overlord

The Allies knew Hitler was expecting some sort of invasion of the French coast. In November 1943, he had written to his military leaders, "Everything indicates that the enemy will launch an offensive against the Western front of Europe, at the latest, in the spring, perhaps even earlier."[1]

The Allies would have to keep the attack a surprise to get past German defenses. Doing so would keep German commanders from knowing where to build up troops and equipment to defeat them.

Early in 1943, the Combined Chiefs of Staff had appointed Lieutenant General Morgan chief of staff to the supreme allied commander, who had not yet been named. Morgan had the job of assembling an organization of British and US personnel to plan the invasion. Morgan named his group COSSAC, using the first letter of each word in his title.

Morgan knew most of the invasion planning had focused only on the amphibious attack until that point. He knew the plan had to be broader:

In our Grand Campaign, our ultimate object is to wage successful war on land in the heart of EUROPE against the main body of the GERMAN strategic reserve. . . . We must plan for the crossing of the beaches, but let us make sure that we get that part of the plan in its right perspective as a passing phase.[2]

By the end of July, COSSAC had written a 113-page plan for the invasion, which Churchill had code-named Operation Overlord.[3] Because the Allies had a shortage of landing craft at this time, the initial version of the plan called for three divisions to attack on a 30-mile (48 km) section of the French coast and another division to land by parachute and glider.[4] COSSAC members took into account factors such as weather, the moon and tides, and beach conditions at the landing sites. All were important to a successful invasion. The area also needed to be close to a port city that could be used

GERMANY'S WRONG GUESSES

Hitler expected the Allies to invade. He could only guess at where they might attack. Hitler told his advisers, "The most suitable landing area, and hence those that are in the most danger, are the two west coast peninsulas of Cherbourg and Brest: they offer very tempting possibilities."[5] Most of Hitler's generals believed an attack would occur at the Pas de Calais. So, they moved their panzer tank forces with this location in mind. Fortunately for the Allies, these guesses were wrong.

to bring in additional troops and equipment once the invasion succeeded.

COSSAC sent men in midget submarines to land on and explore the Normandy coast. They took samples of beach sand to see if it would support the large amount of equipment and troops landing there. The men also surveyed the ocean floor.

Planners eventually selected France's Normandy coast as the best location. Landing there would surprise

CHOOSING NORMANDY

The Allies thought long and hard about where to invade. The Pas de Calais, located on the English Channel coast northwest of Paris, was an attractive area they considered. It contained excellent beaches and several deepwater ports that could be used to offload troops and supplies once they were rebuilt. It was also close to England. Planners rejected an invasion in this area because of the strong German forces and fortifications located there and its vulnerability to counterattack from three directions. The Allies also considered landing in the more remote area of Brittany, but the peninsula was too far from the vital airfields in southern England.

The planners then settled on Normandy as the best site for an invasion. The region was close enough to England for Allied fighter aircraft based there to operate for an extended period of time over the landing area. It was remote enough to isolate it from German reinforcements. Normandy had a deepwater port, Cherbourg, which the Allies could use to land troops and supplies once they captured it and restored it to working condition. But Normandy was hardly perfect. Some of the beaches faced daunting bluffs and could be isolated by flooding. Allied troops would have to negotiate these obstacles as they came ashore.

German forces expecting an attack at the closest point to England, where the channel was narrowest: the Pas de Calais. Normandy could also be more easily isolated from the rest of France than the broader stretches of beach northwest of Paris.

In December 1943, General Eisenhower became commander of Supreme Headquarters, Allied Expeditionary Forces (SHAEF). SHAEF replaced COSSAC, but Morgan remained as Eisenhower's deputy chief of staff. Eisenhower and British general Bernard Montgomery, who had been named as ground forces commander for the invasion of Normandy, examined the draft plan. The two men argued the Allies needed a lot of men for the invasion to succeed. The Allies would have to land divisions—typically 10,000 to 18,000 soldiers—on five beaches from the sea and drop three more divisions from the air.[6] To meet the need for more landing craft, the attack should be delayed until June. The Combined Chiefs of Staff approved these changes. With this decision, the plan was set.

The Big Picture

With their plan in place, the Allies had to prepare for one of the biggest days in military history. Carrying

Matthew Ridgeway, *left*, of the US Army, greets Bernard Montgomery, *right*, while Frederick Morgan watches.

out Operation Overlord would take considerable organization and resources. Many groups collaborated in the effort, which involved devising many smaller operations within the general operation.

The overall plan centered on getting nine divisions of armies from the United States, the United Kingdom, and Canada onto and behind five beaches on the coast of France between the cities of Le Havre and Cherbourg. This was a stretch of approximately 60 miles (97 km). Each division would land on a specific beach that was given a code name. The easternmost beach, closest to

Le Havre, where the British Third Infantry Division would land, was Sword. Moving west, the Canadian Third Infantry Division, supported by elements of Free French and Polish forces, would land on Juno. The British Fiftieth Infantry Division would land on Gold. The US First and Twenty-Ninth Infantry Divisions would come ashore on Omaha. And the US Fourth Infantry Division would land at Utah, closest to Cherbourg, halfway down the Cotentin Peninsula. The British Sixth Airborne and US Eighty-Second and 101st Airborne Divisions would drop behind the beaches to aid in the attack.

Before the troops landed, Allied warships and bombers would attempt to destroy gun emplacements and fortifications. These bombardments would begin at dawn and end just before the seaborne troops were set to land. Once the five beaches had been taken, the Allied forces would push inland while more men arrived to build up the beachhead.

Just as the overall invasion had a code name, so did each portion of the plan. Operation Bolero was the buildup of troops and equipment in the United Kingdom in preparation for the invasion. Operation Bodyguard comprised deception operations to mislead the Germans

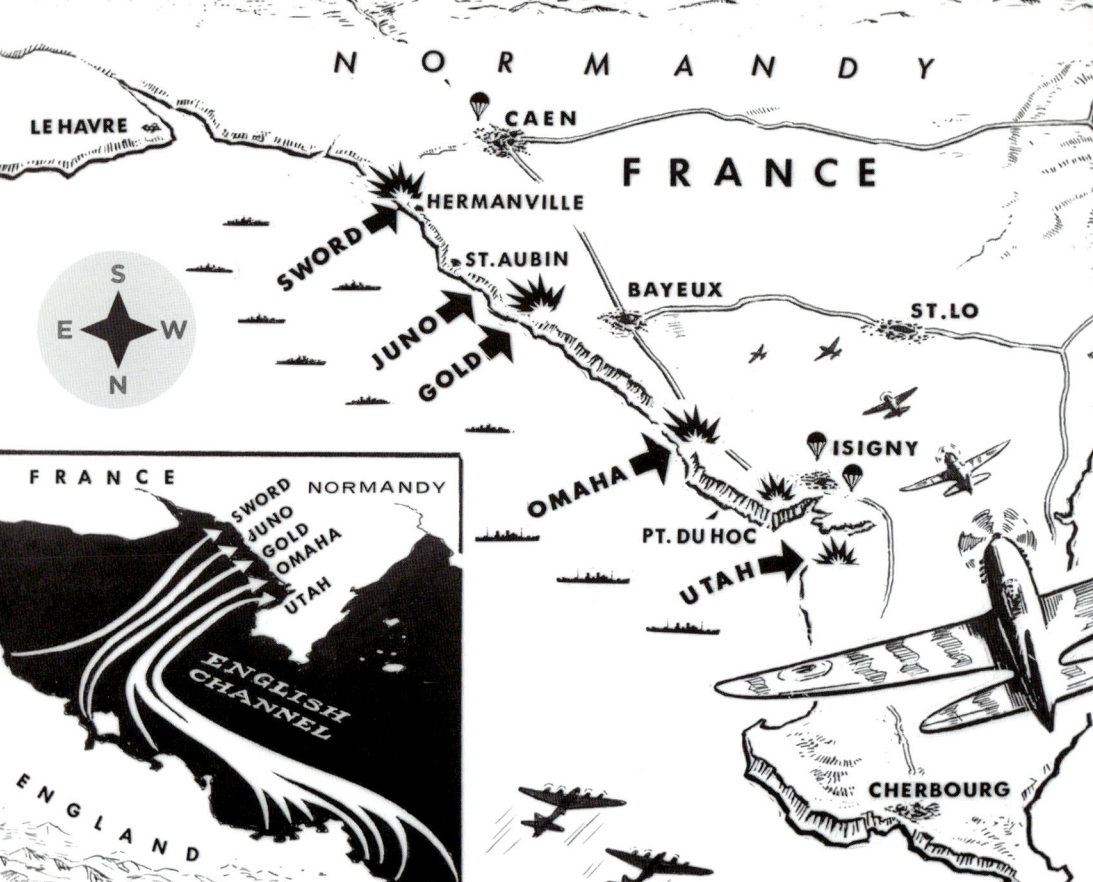

The Allied invasion of Normandy involved ships, planes, and paratroopers, in addition to troops at the five beaches.

and control information. Operation Neptune was the plan for the seaborne landings. The Transportation Plan targeted French railroads and bridges. This would isolate Normandy from the rest of France and make it difficult for the Germans to move forces to counter the invasion once it occurred. Some of the plans were more than 1,000 pages long and weighed more than ten pounds (5 kg).[7]

General Eisenhower was clear about the preparations for Operation Overlord:

> This operation is not being planned with any alternatives. This operation is planned as a victory, and that's the way it's going to be. We're going down there, and we're throwing everything we have into it, and we're going to make it a success.[8]

Operation Bolero

Operation Bolero began in 1942, before specific plans for Operation Overlord had been developed. It required a tremendous movement of resources into the United Kingdom, including soldiers, support personnel, medics, supplies, weapons, and vehicles. Additional airfields had to be constructed all over the United Kingdom to handle the incoming men and materials. In 1942, the British luxury liners *Queen Mary* and *Queen Elizabeth* transported US troops to the United Kingdom across the Atlantic during several voyages.

By June 1944, the Allies had moved 1,536,965 US troops and two and one-half short tons (2.3 metric tons) of equipment to the United Kingdom.[9] Materials included artillery, bulldozers, tanks, trucks, and every kind of supply needed for men and machines to function.

In addition, 7 million short tons (6.4 million metric tons) of oil were stored in the United Kingdom.[10] As D-day drew closer, even more troops and equipment would assemble, ready for the moment when they were told to board ships for France. A fraction of them would land on D-day. The rest would follow.

The Resistance

The French Resistance played an important role in the operation. Started after France surrendered to Germany in 1940, the Resistance helped the Allies by supplying vital intelligence information. It was separate from Free France, which operated in exile. Members also disrupted German communication and supply lines. Called simply the Resistance, this term referred to many anti-German movements. By 1944, the Allied command estimated there were approximately 350,000 members working in France.[11] They were known for their bravery, patriotism, and willingness to sacrifice. Most important, they were behind enemy lines.

Many French had been forced to build German defenses along the coast. They could supply construction information to the Allies. The Resistance also sabotaged

Members of the French Resistance practice drills on March 10, 1944.

railroads, canals, telephones, telegraphs, and factories that made war equipment for the Germans.

The Allies developed two plans for the Resistance to execute on D-day. Plan Vert called for members to place bombs beneath main railroad lines. The bombs could be detonated on D-day and interrupt German train movements to the Normandy beach area. Plan Tortue called for members to block enemy road movements by firing guns into columns of German troops and then running into the woods. The goal was for the Germans to stop their columns to search for the attackers.

Because Germans often captured Resistance members and tortured them for information, the Resistance could not be told the date of the invasion. Instead, Allied forces gave them code phrases that would be broadcast over British Broadcasting

Corporation (BBC) radio to let them know the attack was about to happen and when to carry out their plans.

The Atlantic Wall

To prepare for the expected Allied attack, the Germans built the Atlantic Wall. This series of defensive fortifications stretched from northern Norway to the French border with Spain. Until late 1943, the wall was more boast than reality. But Field Marshall Erwin Rommel energized the construction effort to truly make the wall a defensive measure.

Hitler wanted 15,000 concrete bunkers, manned by 300,000 troops, along the Atlantic coast.[12] In spring 1942, construction began on minefields, concrete walls and bunkers, barbed wire fences, and fortified artillery emplacements. Rommel's improvements included adding minefields to the beaches and placing obstacles between the low- and high-tide marks. He also swamped flood plains and erected poles in fields to keep Allied gliders from landing in them.

The Allies knew details of the German defenses because of the French Resistance and their own reconnaissance missions. Allied forces would have to knock out as many of the concrete-and-steel-reinforced

German soldiers work on a trench in France that connects coastal batteries with barracks and ammunition dumps along the Atlantic Wall.

gun emplacements and bunkers as possible before their troops came ashore. They would also have to contend with the obstacles in the water and on the sand before landing craft could safely beach. All of this would require proper planning and execution.

As the Allies organized D-day, they also carried out plans unrelated to troop and equipment buildups and German defenses. It was an elaborate campaign of deception, and one of the most vital pieces of Operation Overlord.

 14th Army

 XXXI Corps

 XXXIII Corps

 6th Airborne Division

 14th Division

 17th Division

 18th Airborne Division

 21st Airborne Division

 46th Division (variation)

 48th Division

 50th Division

 55th Division

CHAPTER FOUR

DECEIVING THE ENEMY

The Allies knew their best chance for succeeding with Operation Overlord required more than staging an amphibious attack on the beaches of Normandy. They needed to make the Germans think the attack would take place elsewhere, so the Germans would not strengthen their beach defenses at the point of attack.

The Allies also wanted to make their military forces look much larger to the Germans than they actually were. This would keep the Germans guessing whether the Allies would launch a second invasion elsewhere. The Allies would achieve these goals with Operation Fortitude North and Operation Fortitude South. Both were part of the broader project Operation Bodyguard. The two fortitude operations were a joint activity of British and US teams.

Insignias of fake units of the First US Army Group, an imaginary force designed to deceive the Germans

CODE BREAKERS

Allied code breakers helped make Operation Overlord a success by cracking the Enigma, Germany's most common enciphering machine. A cipher substitutes one letter of an alphabet for another. The Enigma was about the size of a small computer with an attached keyboard. The operator typed in a message, which was scrambled by turning the machine's three to five notched wheels with different letters of the alphabet on them. To understand the message, the decoder would have to know the exact setting of these wheels. The Enigma enciphered messages that were particularly hard to break. With the help of the Polish Cipher Bureau, British cryptologists learned to decipher Enigma messages, including the location of German units in France.

Fortitude North

The purpose of Fortitude North was to make Hitler believe the invasion of Europe would take place in Norway. The country was of special concern to Hitler. Germany imported approximately 10 million short tons (9 million metric tons) of iron ore from Sweden each year to use in the production of military items.[1] Germany transported the ore through Norway.

To convince the Germans the invasion would take place by liberating Norway from the Nazis, the Allies made up a fake organization called the British Fourth Army. Early in 1944, a group of British officers traveled to Scotland and began exchanging radio messages that sounded like the radio traffic created by a real army.

To give the appearance of a buildup of planes for an attack, the Allies placed fake bomber aircraft—made of wood and canvas—on airfields in Scotland. They spread rumors about troops being sent to Norway as well.

Operation Fortitude North was a tremendous success. By late spring 1944, Hitler had sent 13 army divisions to Norway, including more than 150,000 naval and air force men.[2] Hitler's commander, Rommel, believed the Allies would attack at Normandy. In May, he requested troops moved to France. Hitler believed the deception about Norway and denied Rommel's request.

Fortitude South

Fortitude South was meant to make the Germans think the Allies would invade at the Pas de Calais. This was France's closest point to England, so the Germans suspected an attack there.

Fortitude South was even more elaborate than its partner plan. Misleading Hitler about the actual invasion site was vital because he already expected an assault on the coast of France. The fictional First US Army Group (FUSAG), led by Lieutenant General George S. Patton Jr., was at the heart of the plan. Eisenhower chose Patton to lead this army because the Germans believed Patton was one of the Allies' best tacticians. Naming him the commander of an invasion force at the Pas de Calais would make Fortitude South even more believable.

To make FUSAG look real to the Germans, the Allies built fake airfields on the English side of the channel, across from the Pas de Calais. The Allied forces also built and displayed fake equipment parks filled with

BEACH JUMPERS

Douglas Fairbanks Jr. was a well-known Hollywood actor in the 1940s. Fairbanks was also a member of the US Navy and had been sent to the United Kingdom in 1942 to learn about naval tactics. There, he learned the British were experimenting with special sound effects as a way to divert the Germans from real landing zones. The British used recordings of noises such as tanks, landing craft, and soldiers' voices to make the Germans think an attack was taking place elsewhere. This protected the real invading Allied troops.

Fairbanks liked the idea so much he convinced the US Navy to allow him to form a special combat group called the Beach Jumpers to imitate large landing forces. Members used landing craft to carry huge speakers to play the recorded sounds, hidden behind clouds of smoke. They also had radio- and radar-jamming equipment to distract Axis radio operators on shore. Balloons carrying radar reflectors and rockets filled with metal strips gave false radar readings. The men also created inflatable human dummies to float in the water to look like assault troops coming ashore. The Beach Jumpers were so successful they earned a presidential unit citation, the highest collective award possible for valor in combat.

tanks and airplanes made of inflated rubber, landing craft and guns made of plywood, huge tent encampments that were left empty, and fake radio antennae. They placed a giant oil pump made of papier-mâché near Dover, next to a phony oil dock built by stagehands from the movie industry. To add realism, a special military unit drove up and down the coast. It broadcast radio transmissions using voices and sound effects that gave the effect of a real army being trained.

But the primary reason Fortitude worked so well was the breaking of the German spy ring in the United Kingdom. By 1944, every German agent in the United Kingdom was actually working for the British.

Fortitude North and South succeeded. By the end of May 1944, the Germans thought the Allies had 89 divisions based in the United Kingdom, when they

DOUBLE AGENTS

German spies in the United Kingdom came to work for the Allies as a result of the British Double Cross system. It was created in 1940. Through it, the British captured and turned many German spies, threatening them with death unless they became double agents pretending to work for Germany but actually working for the Allies. Others turned voluntarily. By the time planning for D-day was taking place, these double agents had spent three years proving themselves to the Allies and could be used for operations Fortitude North and South to spread false information to the Nazis.

really had 47.³ They also believed the Allies had enough landing craft to bring 20 divisions of troops ashore at once, when the Allies had only enough to bring six across the channel at one time.⁴

Keep Out

The final piece of the plan to maintain secrecy and keep accurate information away from the Germans was to control security where real Allied troops were training for the attack. Allies were building many bases in southern England. Eisenhower asked Churchill to ban all visitors there. Eisenhower worried about spies reaching the area and reporting back to Hitler. Churchill refused, not wanting to upset the lives of civilians nearby. Eventually, Churchill gave in and had all visitors banned from the area.

While Operation Bodyguard was busy misleading Hitler and his armies, preparations for the real invasion were under way. They included people near and far, from the training areas of the United Kingdom to factories in the United States.

Supreme Headquarters
ALLIED EXPEDITIONARY FORCE
Office of the Secretary General Staff

3 February 1944

MEMORANDUM FOR: Chief of Staff.

Subject: Precise of Plan "BODYGUARD"

1. Plan "BODYGUARD" is an overall deception policy for the war against Germany, approved by the Combined Chiefs of Staff (TAB A). Its object is to induce the enemy to make faulty strategic dispositions in relation to operations by the United Nations against Germany.

2. This overall deception policy is presented to induce the enemy to believe that the allied plan for 1944 is as follows:

Long range bomber reinforcement is delaying ground forces build-up;
An attack on Northern Norway with Russia is to be concerted in the Spring;
The main Allied effort in Spring 1944 should be against the Balkans
Operations in Italy would be continued, augmented by amphibious operations.

3. In regard to Allied strength and dispositions, we should induce the enemy to believe the following:

Shortage of manpower has obliged cannibalisation within the British Army in UK;
Number of divisions in UK is less than is in fact the case;
Personnel of certain allied divisions in Mediterranean are being relieved by fresh divisions from U.S.;
Shortage of landing craft exists until Summer, 1944;
Forces in Mediterranean are greater than is, in fact, the case;
French forces are taking over responsibility for defense of North Africa, relieving Anglo-American forces for Spring operations elsewhere;
British divisions and craft are being transferred from India to Middle East;
Fresh divisions from U.S. are expected to arrive in Mediterranean.

4. Means of implementation of plan "BODYGUARD" include movement of forces, camouflage devices, W/T deception, diplomatic approaches to Sweden and Turkey, leakage and rumours, and political warfare.

ROBERT E. BAKER,
Major, G.S.C.,
Asst. Sec. General Staff.

A memorandum relating to Operation Bodyguard

CHAPTER FIVE

GEARING UP

Landing six infantry divisions on the beaches of Normandy and three more airborne divisions inland for Operation Overlord would require a great deal of equipment. The Allies would need ships and landing craft, trucks, tanks, artillery, and jeeps, as well as aircraft to drop bombs on German positions.

Higgins's Contribution

Andrew Higgins was responsible for designing and building the landing craft, vehicle and personnel (LCVP) that would carry many of the troops and equipment from ships anchored in the channel to the beaches. Higgins was a boat builder in Louisiana. He believed the US Navy was going to need thousands of small boats during the war that could navigate in shallow waters. He anticipated steel might be in short supply and designed a landing craft made of wood. It had a front ramp that could be lowered as the craft approached the beach to allow the troops and equipment to be unloaded

Andrew Higgins, *on chair*, talks to sailors attending his two-week class on how to operate and repair amphibious craft.

quickly and easily. His design was better than anything the US Navy had drafted, so he was awarded the contract to build the landing craft for the Allies.

Higgins built more than 20,000 LCVPs during the war.[1] They were called Higgins boats. They were used in France, as well as in the Pacific and the Mediterranean. Their most important moment would be on D-day. These craft were vital to the invasion.

HIGGINS BOATS

The Higgins boat was 36 feet, 3 inches (11 m) long and 10 feet, 10 inches (3.3 m) wide. Its ramp was made of metal, and the sides and stern were made of plywood. These boats could carry 36 fully equipped soldiers or 8,000 pounds (3,629 kg) of cargo.[2] Two machine guns were mounted near the back of the boat.

The boat did not provide a smooth ride. Even in relatively calm waters, it bounced and shook, and water came over the sides. But the Higgins boat was fast. It could bring a small platoon of soldiers to shore and discharge them in seconds before returning to the transport ship for another group. A platoon could number between 16 and 40 men.[3] The largest platoons would have to be reorganized into "boat sections" to fit in the landing craft.[4]

Higgins was very good at mass-producing his boats. He paid his workers top wages and operated multiple factory assembly lines in the New Orleans, Louisiana, area. Some of these factories were simply glorified tents with canvas roofs. His workforce of 30,000 was unusually integrated for the time, including African Americans and women.[5] Higgins and his staff were so important to victory that 20 years after D-day Eisenhower stated, "Andrew Higgins is the man who won the war for us."[6]

The Allies needed other types of vessels for the invasion, too. Higgins built many of them. They included the landing ship, tank (LST); landing craft, tank (LCT); landing craft, personnel, large (LCPL); landing craft, mechanized (LCM); landing craft, infantry (LCI); and supply vessels. The LST was crucial. At 327 feet (100 m) long, it was a big ship. The LST had a flat bottom, which made it hard to control in waves. But it was helpful for landing on shallow beaches and discharging dozens of trucks and tanks in a single load. It had doors that opened on the sides and a ramp that could be lowered to allow vehicles to drive ashore. These various vehicles would get men and equipment from the Allied ships that sailed from England to the beaches, for the invasion and afterward, as the Allies established themselves in France.

SLAPTON SANDS

On April 28, 1944, the Allies were conducting Exercise Tiger on Slapton Sands, a stretch of beach on the south coast of England that closely resembled Utah Beach. Exercise Tiger was a training exercise using eight LSTs to prepare for D-day. As the LSTs moved through the water, nine German boats suddenly appeared and launched torpedoes, hitting three of the vessels. One of the LSTs made it into port. The other two were destroyed, with a total of 749 American soldiers dead or missing.[7] Because of the secrecy surrounding D-day, the attack was covered up so the Germans could not link the training to the Normandy invasion.

More Marvels

Boats were not the only innovation used during World War II and D-day especially. One of the most dangerous parts of the plan to land troops on the beaches of Normandy were the defenses the Germans had put there. The Allies needed specialized vehicles that could support the first troops as they reached the beaches. Major General Percy Hobart of the United Kingdom oversaw the development of many specialized tanks that would come to be known as "Hobart's Funnies."[8]

The Allies also relied on a US tank known as the duplex drive, or DD. This was a Sherman tank equipped with a waterproof canvas screen and propellers that allowed it to be launched at sea from landing craft, where it would slowly swim to the beach. Once ashore, the crew could deflate the screen so the tank could act as a regular fighting vehicle.

Other innovations included a modified Sherman tank code-named Crab and called the flail. It had a spinning drum with weighted chains (the flail) on the front. As the tank crawled across the sand, the rotating chains exploded enemy mines.

A Crab, or flail, tank protected troops by exploding mines.

The Bobbin tank could lay down huge carpets of reinforced fabric matting over soft ground. This allowed other vehicles to traverse the area without bogging down. Fascine tanks carried bundles of wooden poles that could be dumped into ditches to fill them in so vehicles could travel across. Arks carried 30-foot (9 m) metal bridges, folded in half and sticking straight into the air, that could be quickly unfolded and used over ditches or small streams. And the Crocodile was a flame-throwing tank. It towed a trailer with 400 gallons (1,514 L) of fuel it could use to shoot flames 80 to 120 yards (73 to 110 m).

Another piece of technology needed for the success of Operation Overlord was a project called Pipeline Under the Ocean, or PLUTO. Once they reached France, the Allies were going to need gas for their tanks, trucks, jeeps, and ambulances. The British manufactured three-inch- (8 cm) thick lead pipe in sections. They welded the sections together and wound them around huge floating cylinders. The sections could be unwound along the bottom of the channel to create a pipeline for fuel. The Allies laid 17 PLUTO

GERMANY'S FIGHTER PLANES AND FAST BOATS

The Germans had new equipment of their own, including the ME-262 fighter. It could fly faster than any Allied plane. But Hitler wanted to bomb London, not defend Germany, so he ordered Professor Willy Messerschmitt to build the ME-262 as a bomber. Messerschmitt tried, but he could not get the technology right. The aircraft was eventually used as a fighter plane and did well. One squadron took down 25 Allied bombers and five fighters in one encounter without losing a single plane.[9] But it was too late in the war to make a difference.

What the Germans did have were *schnell*, or "fast," boats, known simply as S-boats. The British referred to them as E-boats. The *E* was for enemy. S-boats were similar in size to US patrol boats known as PTs. S-boats could lay mines and fire torpedoes, but they were ineffective as fighting ships. Overall, the Germans did not have enough air or naval equipment to effectively battle the Allies on the seas or in the skies over Normandy on D-day.

pipelines that pumped more than 150 million gallons (568 million L) of fuel.[10]

A final innovation for the invasion was Mulberry, or temporary, harbors. Once the troops landed in Normandy, the Allies would send additional supplies that could not be left on the beaches without being swamped by incoming tides. Capturing a French port that was heavily defended by the Germans would be time consuming. The Allies designed two of these artificial harbors to meet their immediate needs until a port could be taken.

Preparing the Troops

Finally, as the day of the invasion neared, the soldiers who would carry out Operation Overlord had to be brought together and prepared. They came to assembly areas called "sausages," named for their shape on maps: long and narrow like a sausage.[11] The sausages had tents and were camouflaged from German planes with netting. The soldiers were fenced in and not allowed to leave for fear the attack plans might be leaked to the enemy.

The men were issued new uniforms that had been soaked with a chemical that would protect them from poisonous gas. The chemical kept the fabric from breathing. This made the soldiers sweaty and smelly. The men hated them. Private Edward Jeziorski of the US Army's 507th Parachute Infantry said, "They were the lousiest, the coldest, the clammiest, the stiffest, the stinkiest articles of clothing that were ever dreamed up to be worn by individuals."[12] The soldiers also received new weapons and escape aids to use in case they were captured. These included metal files, silk scarves printed with a map of France, water-purifying tablets, and French money.

The week before the invasion launch, the soldiers were briefed about the plan of attack. Sand tables and huge models of the Normandy area made of sponge rubber showed the geography and terrain of the area and where the landings would take place. They also indicated buildings, roads, bridges, obstacles, and fortifications in great detail. These 3-D maps were intended to give the troops

ASSEMBLING IN ENGLAND

Soldiers and sailors began assembling in southern England at the beginning of May 1944. They came on transport ships and LSTs, sailing down from Ireland in formations of 20, 40, and even 100 ships. They also came by train, bus, truck, or foot from the northern areas of the country. Almost 2 million men gathered in southern England, serving as either troops or support staff to cook and provide other services to the soldiers.[13]

US troops and vehicles board ships at Brixham, England, preparing to invade Normandy.

a clear idea of where they would land, what to expect, and what their movements would be.

The Allies gathered equipment at the sausages, too. They filled fields and vacant lots with tanks, spotter aircraft, guns, artillery, gasoline, food, water, and anything else that might be needed during the invasion. All equipment was covered with a greasy substance called Cosmoline that would protect it from salt water.

The stage was set, the men were outfitted and trained, and the equipment was ready. Everyone waited, poised for the command to go.

CHAPTER SIX

LOADING AND LAUNCHING

Everything was ready. The date for D-day had been set: June 5, 1944. On May 31, the Allies began loading all the men and equipment that had been staged in various parts of England. Everything was on the move.

Troops were loaded onto LSTs and other transport boats to ferry them out to larger ships anchored in the channel. Almost 3,000 ships from 12 countries waited.[1] Lieutenant Ralph Eastridge of the US Army's 115th Regiment, Twenty-Ninth Division, commented on the scene:

> We were side by side with so many crafts that a man could have jumped from one deck to another for a half mile or more. Toward the sea, we could see destroyers and larger ships at anchor. The harbor was just jammed with boats.[2]

Men board an LCVP to ferry from port to transport vessels offshore before heading across the English Channel to invade Normandy.

As the troops boarded their ships, each received a copy of the order issued by Eisenhower. In it, he wrote,

> The eyes of the world are upon you. The hopes and prayers of liberty-loving people everywhere march with you. . . . Your task will not be an easy one. Your enemy is well trained, well equipped, and battle-hardened, he will fight savagely. But this is the year 1944! . . . The tide has turned! The free men of the world are marching together to Victory! I have full confidence in your courage, devotion to duty, and skill in battle. We will accept nothing less than full Victory! Good luck![3]

Everything was ready to go, but the morning of June 4 was stormy. The weather would prevent the Allied bombers and navy ships from bombarding the German positions the next day before the men landed. And the landing craft carrying the troops might sink in the rough seas. Eisenhower decided to postpone Operation Overlord until June 6. The troops had to remain on their ships. Eisenhower did not think there was time to take them back to

A PAUSE IN THE STORM

The bad weather on June 4 forced Eisenhower to decide whether the invasion would take place on June 6 or be postponed for two weeks. On June 5, the bad weather continued, but Eisenhower received a report the storm would ease the next day. Based on that, he said, "Okay, let's go," giving the final order to launch Operation Overlord.[4]

Dwight D. Eisenhower met with US paratroopers in England before they boarded aircraft headed to Normandy for the invasion.

shore and reload for the June 6 landing. Many of the men became miserably seasick waiting on the rough seas.

Paratroopers First

Before the ground troops could make their assault on the beaches of Normandy, airborne units would land inland to secure the flanks, or sides, of the invasion zone. The pathfinders would go first. These were paratroopers, soldiers dropped from transport aircraft into an enemy area to mark and set up landing zones for others who would follow. They would use automatic direction-finder radios as well as light beacons to mark the drop zones.

On the stormy night of June 5–6, the airborne units began their mission. However, only some of the pathfinders found and marked the proper drop zones. More than 13,000 paratroopers were dropped during the D-day invasion, but not always successfully.[5] The continuing cloud cover made it difficult for the airplanes to drop the troopers in the correct locations, or from a high-enough altitude, and many paratroopers were injured when they hit the ground. Some paratroopers were immediately hit by German ground fire. Soldiers

USING GLIDERS

The Allies used two types of wooden gliders during World War II: the British Horsa and the US Waco. The Horsa was made entirely out of wood and had a wingspan of 88 feet (27 m). The Waco spanned 84 feet (26 m) and had a steel and canvas fuselage and a wooden floor.

The gliders were lightweight yet carried several thousand pounds of cargo, such as several soldiers, a jeep with a driver, or a small field gun with ammunition and two artillerymen. A powered airplane would tow a glider on a 300-foot (91 m) rope to get it off the ground. Gliders had the advantage of being cheaper than powered airplanes. They also did not require a landing strip and could instead land in spaces such as cow pastures. By February 1944, the United States had shipped 2,100 gliders to England.[6] Almost all of them were destroyed on D-day, but they were designed to be expendable.

became separated and lost. Small groups of Allied troops joined together wherever they could. They often became a mix of men from different units and in locations far from where they were supposed to be. Some drowned when they landed in the channel or in rivers, too loaded down with equipment to swim.

However, by dawn, groups of paratroopers were cutting telephone wires and knocking down telephone poles, quickly disrupting the German lines of communication. They also captured the town of Sainte Mère Église, as planned, which allowed them to control the main highway from Caen to Cherbourg. British paratroopers attacked the German artillery battery at Merville and destroyed it. Allied glider planes began coming in behind enemy lines. The planes delivered equipment such as jeeps and pack howitzers to reinforce the lightly armed paratroopers.

OPERATION TITANIC

Operation Titanic was another ploy by the Allies to deceive the Germans. On June 5 and 6, 1944, Allied forces dropped 500 paradummies in four zones to make the Germans think the invasion was taking place somewhere other than the real location.[7] These life-size bodies were designed to look like paratroopers. They were made of burlap cloth stuffed with straw or of inflatable rubber. The paradummies successfully distracted part of the German army from the real beach landings.

With so many paratroopers scattered over such a wide area, German commanders were confused about what was happening.

German forces struggled to get to the beaches. In addition to losing control of the main highway from Caen to Cherbourg, they were occupied by fighting the paratroopers and confused about where the actual invasion was taking place. The Germans also overestimated the size of the invading force, which worked in the Allies' favor.

Preparing for the Infantry

The three airborne divisions had more work to do. They had to secure the flanks of the invasion area. They also worked to disrupt and confuse the German army so it would be less likely to mount a large counterattack on the beaches when the ground troops arrived. The British Sixth Airborne Division captured or destroyed the bridges along the Dives River and Canal, securing the eastern flank of the invasion

"As dawn broke, we could observe one of the most impressive sights of any wartime action. Wave after wave of medium and light bombers could be seen sweeping down the invasion beaches to drop their bombs."[8]
—Captain Shettle of the US 506th Parachute Infantry Regiment

zone. The US Eighty-Second and 101st Airborne Divisions dropped behind Utah Beach to secure the causeways, the roads over the flooded ground that connected the beach with the rest of the Cotentin Peninsula. Airborne troopers destroyed some bridges and captured others without destroying them.

The Allies put a great deal of faith in air bombardment and naval gunfire to destroy German beach fortifications. But the plan did not work as devised. The heavy bombers targeting the Germans on Omaha Beach flew above the clouds and could not see their targets. They delayed releasing their bombs for fear of hitting their own ships in the channel. As a result, the bombardment completely missed the German beach defenses.

On Utah Beach, medium bombers coming in under the clouds could see their targets and were highly effective in destroying German emplacements

> "ALERTE! A great number of low flying planes fly over the town—shaving the rooftops, it is like a thunderous noise, suddenly, the alarm is given, there is a fire in town. In the meantime, the Germans fire all they can at the planes.
> We go into hiding, what is going on? Thousands of paratroopers are landing everywhere amid gun fire. We are huddled in M. Besselievre's garage with our friends. Our liberators are here!"[9]
> —M. Andre Mace, resident of Sainte Mère Église, describing in his diary what he saw on June 6, 1944

D-DAY: THE NORMANDY INVASION • 67

> "We could hear . . . planes . . . then no sounds . . . followed by . . . swishing noises . . . the tearing of branches . . . followed by loud crashes and intermittent screams. The gliders were coming in rapidly . . . from different directions. Many overshot the field and landed in the surrounding woods, while others crashed into nearby farmhouses and stone walls. . . . Equipment broke away and catapulted as it hit the ground, plowing up huge mounds of earth. Bodies and bundles were scattered the length of the field."[12]
> —Private John Fitzgerald, US Army, 502nd Parachute Infantry Regiment, 101st Airborne Division, describing a glider landing

on the beach. The short naval gunfire bombardment missed hitting German fortifications, but they did clear big pieces of minefields.

Allied forces flew more than 14,000 missions on D-day.[10] The Luftwaffe flew approximately 250 missions.[11] Most targeted the Allied ships on the edges of the invasion.

The Allied paratroopers and gliders had landed, and the ships and bombers had done their tasks. It was time for the amphibious part of the invasion: bringing the men ashore.

Gliders and parachutes are scattered across a field in France. The body of the gliders is meant to detach and is not broken from crashing.

CHAPTER SEVEN

GOING ASHORE

As the paratroopers and glider forces overhead did their work, the first ships moved into the Normandy area to clear mines. The Allied forces controlled the airspace above land and water. The Germans had blanketed the area between the Isle of Wight and the French coast with as many mines as they could. It was really the only naval defense they had there.

Allied ships filled the waters off the beaches. Allied forces patrolled the channel against German U-boats. Operation Cork consisted of boats laying mines to force enemy ships away from the invasion armada. It also included air and sea patrols to prevent German aircraft and ships from interfering with the invasion.

Minesweeping ships cleared the mines from a wide path in the channel and in the shallow landing areas off the beaches. A few ships hit mines off of Utah Beach, but overall, the invasion armada made the voyage from England to France without meeting serious resistance.

Allied troops aboard a transport ship await evacuation before the vessel capsizes and sinks.

Landing

The bombardment groups included battleships, cruisers, and destroyers. They aligned themselves behind the men approaching the beaches in LCVPs and other landing craft, ready to start firing above the troops at 5:50 a.m. As the Allied bombers did their work overhead, the men in the boats kept waiting for the Germans to fire back, but it was ominously quiet. A reporter for the *Saturday Evening Post* magazine, Martin Sommers, was standing on board the USS *McCook* off Omaha Beach. He described the Allied bombing as it increased in intensity:

> Thunderous explosions rolled along the shore, followed by high bursts of multicolored flak, and then a geyser of flame here, another there. . . . The blasts were coming so fast that they merged into one roar. The shoreline became a broken necklace of flame.[2]

THE OLD LADIES

The six US and British battleships used in the Normandy invasion were nicknamed the "old ladies" because each was between 18 and 29 years old.[1] Some of them had been scheduled for demolition when the war broke out. These ships were used because they were too slow to participate in fleet operations against the Axis navies. One of the US battleships, the USS *Nevada*, had been heavily damaged by the Japanese during the attack on Pearl Harbor. The navy renovated it and sent it to Normandy to take part in the D-day invasion.

An Allied ship, the HMS *Holmes*, shells the Germans in Normandy on June 6, 1944.

Next, the Allied naval ships began firing. The Germans fired back. Every ship in the Allied battle fleet opened fire until 6:20 a.m., when the cease-fire order was given. They had fired on every German pillbox, fortified position, and house that might hide German guns. But the 30-minute bombardment was not enough to destroy all the German defenses. The infantry that would soon land would have to deal with the remaining defenses.

The Germans were shocked to find themselves suddenly being bombed from above and fired on from the sea. German private Franz Gockel recalled,

> *The sea came alive. Assault boats and landing craft were rapidly approaching the beach. A comrade stumbled out of the smoke and dust to my position and screamed, "Watch out! They're coming!"*[3]

After the minesweepers did their job, the LCTs moved in to bring tanks to the beaches. The LCTs were clearly marked with letters indicating where they were intended to land: *O* for Omaha, *U* for Utah, and so on.[4] The DD tanks unloaded in the channel and used their propellers to swim to shore. Because of the rough seas off of Omaha, 32 of the 36 tanks launched into the channel sank.[5] Their crews drowned. On the British beaches, LCT captains decided to ferry the tanks all the way to the beach, even under German fire. The tanks that succeeded in landing opened fire on the German concrete bunkers.

Reaching the Beaches

The first wave of landing craft, mostly Higgins boats, reached the beaches, handicapped a little by strong offshore winds and currents that threw many of them off course. As the men began leaving the boats, they discovered in most areas the bombings from the air and naval groups had not taken out as many German defenses as planned. This was in part because the Germans had constructed their Atlantic Wall so well, but also because the heavy bombers mostly missed their targets. The bombs targeting Omaha fell inland, killing cows but leaving the German troops unharmed.

The troops in their Higgins boats were scheduled to land in four waves. The first was the swimming tanks and Higgins boats carrying assault teams of 30 men

MINES AND MINESWEEPERS

The Germans used a variety of mines, including contact, antenna, and pressure. Contact mines exploded when they came into contact with anything. Antenna mines were located below the surface, with a long wire that was attached to a float. When a metal object touched the wire, it would detonate the mine. Some of the German mines floated and others were attached to the seafloor. Pressure mines exploded when there was a change in the water pressure created by the hull of a passing ship.

Allied minesweepers aimed to disarm or set off mines and keep them from harming other vehicles or troops. After a minesweeping ship cut a cable, the mine would bob to the surface. There, gunfire would detonate it. Minesweepers also had an electric system designed to reduce their magnetic field. This kept the ships from setting off magnetic mines, which would be deactivated from a distance by another device that did project a magnetic field. To set off acoustic, or sound-detonated, mines, minesweeping ships had a machine that made a hammer-like sound.

Landing craft rush US soldiers to Normandy's beaches.

each.[6] Five minutes later, the second wave would land with more troops, plus combat engineers and demolition teams that would destroy German beach obstacles to open a path for reinforcements. Ten minutes after that, the third wave would land with more infantry and bulldozer tanks. After another two minutes, the final wave would launch with more combat engineers.

The timing was not as precise as scheduled because of the stormy weather, which created strong tides, high winds, and big waves, plus cover from smoke created by Allied smokescreens and grass fires sparked by the bombings. Some boats hit mines and exploded. Others landed in the wrong place. But the commanders on the beach adapted to the circumstances, and the troops showed initiative and the motivation to make the invasion work. Working together, these men proceeded to attack the five beaches.

BEACH OBSTACLES

The Allies coped with myriad obstacles placed on the beaches by the Germans. Belgian gates were iron gates ten feet (3 m) high that sat in a line in the water off shore. Teller mines were antitank mines with dynamite, attached to the gates or other structures. Heavy logs driven into the sand at an angle facing the sea had Teller mines lashed to them. Hedgehogs were three or four steel rails six feet (1.8 m) long welded together in a shape like a giant jack. They blocked landing craft from coming ashore.

CHAPTER EIGHT

BEACH BY BEACH

Operation Overlord was not a single assault on a single location. What took place on D-day varied according to the beach where the Allies landed.

Utah

Three miles (5 km) wide, Utah was the most northwesterly of the Normandy beaches. The US Army Fourth Infantry Division landed there. The tanks and Higgins boats came ashore approximately one mile (2 km) south of their intended landing zone. This was good luck, because this part of the beach was not as heavily defended. US medium bombers had destroyed the main German fortification in the area.

The Allied commanders on the beach had to quickly adjust to the situation, which was nothing like the sand table displays provided in England. The commanders could try to move their troops to the original landing zone or simply proceed from where they were. Colonel James van Fleet, commander of the Eighth Infantry

US troops carry their equipment onto Utah Beach during the successful Allied invasion of Normandy on June 6, 1944.

US soldiers inspect radio-operated German beetle tanks captured on Utah Beach.

Regiment, said, "I made the decision. 'Go straight inland,' I ordered. 'We've caught the enemy at a weak point, so let's take advantage of it.'"[1]

The demolition teams came in to clear the beach of obstacles and allow more tanks and vehicles to follow. They also blew holes in the seawall. At the same time, troops were landing in Higgins boats and firing back at the Germans. The men followed the tanks through the open seawall and headed inland. There was almost a bottleneck of men and tanks and vehicles.

As the tanks moved through the seawall, they fired on more German fortifications. Soon, they were moving along the causeways spanning the flooded coastal plain. The infantry moved inland toward Sainte Mère Église. There, they would meet infantry soldiers of the Eighty-Second Airborne Division who had already captured the town.

Utah Beach did not have the formidable German defenses of other locations. A second-class German division defended the beach. The Allies took the beach by midday. In total, 20,000 men and 1,700 military vehicles came ashore there on D-day.[2] There were approximately 200 US casualties, well below the worst-case predictions.[3]

Omaha

Omaha Beach was the most difficult area for the Allies to take. It was the only sand beach between Gold and Utah Beaches. Therefore, it was an obvious landing place for an Allied invasion. Six miles (10 km) across, Omaha was lined with bluffs. They gave the Germans an immense defensive advantage. The First and Twenty-Ninth US Army infantry divisions assigned to come ashore there would not have an easy time.

Because it was such an obvious landing place, the Germans had put many defensive measures in place—

> "Face downward, as far as eyes could see in either direction, were the huddled bodies of men living, wounded, and dead, as tightly packed together as a layer of cigars in a box. . . . Everywhere, the frantic cry, 'Medics, hey, Medics' could be heard above the horrible din."[6]
>
> —Major Charles Tegtmeyer, surgeon, Sixteenth Infantry Regiment, US First Division

more than at the other beaches. Defenses included tank traps, mines, and heavily fortified gun emplacements on the cliffs called resistance nests. The Germans also had a series of trenches where they could move between gun batteries without exposing themselves to gunfire.

The Allied plan was for the infantry to land at the same time as amphibious Sherman tanks, which would give them plenty of firepower. But only four of three dozen tanks arrived on the beach.[4] And many men landed in the wrong place, units became mixed up, and no one was sure just who was supposed to be doing what. Omaha Beach is remembered as "bloody Omaha" because so many US troops died there as they tried to reach the protection of the cliffs.[5]

Private George Roach was an assistant flamethrower operator. He described his experience:

> We went down the ramp and the casualty rate was very bad. We couldn't determine where the fire was coming from, whether from the top of the bluff or from the

summer beach-type homes on the shore. I just dropped myself into the sand and took my rifle and fired it at this house and Sergeant Wilkes asked, "What are you firing at?" and I said, "I don't know."[7]

Two battalions of the elite US Army Rangers were tasked with getting rid of a battery of German howitzer guns located between Omaha and Utah Beaches at Pointe du Hoc.[8] These guns had a range of 14 miles (23 km) and threatened the Allied forces on both beaches. The Ranger battalions had to scale 100-foot (30 m) cliffs to reach the battery. They used ladders and rocket-propelled grappling hooks attached to ropes to climb the cliffs. Germans dropped grenades from above and cut some of the Rangers' ropes. Still, the Rangers made it to the top in five minutes and drove off the Germans, only to discover the guns were not there. The Rangers found the howitzers a short distance away and destroyed them.

DEADLY DECISION

As US forces stormed Omaha, they could have been aided by some of the tanks Hobart developed for the war. For some unknown reason, Lieutenant General Omar Bradley turned down the British offer to provide most of these vehicles to US units. The Americans accepted the DD tank, but not the other types, which would have saved lives on Omaha and Utah had they been used.

> **SLEEPING THROUGH D-DAY**
>
> Hitler was asleep when the Germans received word of the invasion at Normandy. Some sources say Hitler was not awakened because his commanders thought the invasion was only a diversion. Others thought they were afraid to wake Hitler, who slept until nearly noon that day. Because only Hitler could order the panzer tank divisions to move, these forces were later getting to the battle than they could or should have been.

Other Ranger units helped lead the Americans off the beach while US Navy destroyers came in as closely as they could and focused their fire on the German positions. Small-unit commanders led their men up the bluffs to take advantage of gaps in the German defenses. They destroyed enemy strong points one by one from behind. By nightfall, the Allies had managed to take the beach and make some headway inland. Of the 34,000 troops who landed on Omaha, 2,400 were killed or wounded.[9]

Gold

Gold Beach was five miles (8 km) long and the geographic center of the Allied invasion beaches. The British army was in charge of landing there. They found the preceding Allied airstrikes had taken out many of the German defenses. However, exceptionally high tides covered the beach with water. This prevented the

Allies from seeing the antitank obstacles and mines there and defusing them. So, many of the first landing craft to make shore were damaged. But the British were able to take control of Gold in a few hours, with 400 casualties.[10]

Juno

At Juno, Canadian forces had the primary goal of moving inland, seizing Carpiquet Airfield, severing the Caen–Bayeux road, and linking Gold and Sword Beaches. But the troops had problems before they even landed. Again, the tide was higher than planned. The

MULBERRY HARBOR

After the initial invasion, the Allies constructed a Mulberry harbor at the western end of Gold Beach, near Arromanches. They assembled it from pieces that had been built in the United Kingdom and towed across the channel. The Allies erected one at Omaha, too, but it was destroyed two weeks later in heavy storms.

A Mulberry harbor consisted of a breakwater, or pier, made from concrete caissons and old warships that were sunk to form a shelter for cargo ships as they docked. They were connected to the shore with a series of floating roadways.

A fleet of ships was needed to tow the two harbors across the channel. The harbors were a vital staging area for Allied supply ships, providing equipment and materials for the Allies once the beachheads had been secured. In the first 109 days of the invasion, 2,500,000 troops, more than 500,000 vehicles, and 680 million cubic feet (19 million cu m) of equipment and supplies would move ashore through the Mulberry harbors.[11]

water hid the German obstacles on the beach. Mines and obstacles damaged or ruined approximately 30 percent of the landing craft.¹² Many soldiers had to wade ashore, making them more vulnerable to attack. And the air and naval bombardments had not damaged German defenses as much as the Allies had hoped they would.

Once the Canadian troops made it to the German defenses, they were able to overcome them quickly. By the end of the day, the Canadians and Poles had advanced farther than forces on any other beach. Still, they were short of their planned objectives. Of the 21,400 men who landed on Juno, 1,200 were killed or wounded.¹³

Sword

Sword was the farthest east of the five D-day beaches and only nine miles (14 km) from Caen, which was critical to the Allied invasion. All the main roads in the area ran through Caen. If the Allies were to successfully move inland from Normandy, they would need to control the city.

The beach was not heavily defended. An hour after landing, the British had control of it. In the afternoon, parts of a German panzer division launched a serious

The Mulberry harbor is alive with activity as troops unload supplies for the Allies at Colleville-sur-Mer, France.

counterattack, but Allied fighter-bombers destroyed many of the German tanks and stopped the advance. The British would not take Caen on D-day, but they made a foothold on Sword Beach.

When D-day was over, Allied forces had established a lodgment area 60 miles (97 km) wide and several miles deep. The cost in lives was high, as the beaches were covered with blood and dead bodies. There were 10,000 Allied casualties, 4,413 of them deaths.[14] German casualties are not known and are estimated at 4,000 to 9,000.[15] The Allies had achieved their goal of securing a foothold in Normandy, laying the groundwork for the liberation of France and the end of Hitler's regime.

CHAPTER NINE

THE NEXT DAY AND BEYOND

Operation Overlord's first day was a success. The Allies now had a foothold in France, though it was uncertain. The Allies would take several days to link all five beaches into one stronghold. And the battle with the German forces and the panzer counterattacks would last several more weeks. But as the morning of June 7 dawned, more Allied troops, equipment, and supplies were waiting offshore to begin unloading. Even more were awaiting transport from England to France.

Allied forces then fought to consolidate control of the beachhead and create a sufficient lodgment area to support a drive across France toward Germany. They were going to attack Hitler on a new front and force him to pull resources away from the Eastern Front, as Stalin had urged.

Landing ships fill the waters at Normandy's shore while men and vehicles make their way onto the beaches and beyond.

CASUALTIES STATISTICS

Normandy campaign casualties numbered in the hundreds of thousands. More than 425,000 troops in all—Allied and German— were dead, hurt, or missing. The Allies suffered more than 209,000 casualties, including almost 37,000 ground force deaths and 16,714 air force deaths. Of the Allied casualties, 125,847 were US ground forces and 83,045 were from the Twenty-First Army Group, which consisted of British, Canadian, and Polish ground forces.

The Germans also suffered greatly. Approximately 200,000 German servicemen were killed or wounded.

Civilian lives were also lost. Between 15,000 and 20,000 French civilians died during the Normandy campaign.[1]

While D-day was a tremendous victory, the Allies had much more fighting to do in the larger campaign to take Normandy. The Normandy invasion was only the beginning of a push that would end the war. The stretch of territory held by the Allies was approximately 56 miles (90 km) wide, with several gaps between beaches that ranged from three to 12 miles (5 to 19 km). These gaps were of vital concern to Allied commanders. But the Germans were unable to take advantage of them. Their mobile armored formations had been kept near Paris. They now found it difficult to get to Normandy as a result of the Allied airstrikes on the rail network.

The Germans in Normandy were nearly isolated from the rest of their army in France. And the Allies and their air support could slow the movement of German troops and equipment into the area with fighter bomber attacks. German convoys could only move during the few hours of the short northern European summer nights.

Moving Inland

On June 29, US forces captured the French city of Cherbourg, an important port on the channel. The Germans had destroyed the docks and port facilities. It would take months to put them back into operation. Meanwhile, the Germans dug into the hedgerows of the Cotentin Peninsula and fought for every field and village in the area. For a time, it seemed the Allied drive inland would stall.

> "I noticed that nothing moved on the beach except one bulldozer. The beach was covered with debris, sunken craft, and wrecked vehicles. We saw many bodies in the water. . . . We jumped into chest-high water and waded ashore. Then, we saw that the beach was literally covered with the bodies of American soldiers wearing the blue and gray patches of the 29th Infantry Division."[2]
> —Lieutenant Horace Henderson, Sixth Engineer Special Brigade, describing Omaha Beach on June 7

In July, six weeks after the invasion, the Allies were still bottlenecked in an area of Normandy roughly 50 miles (80 km) wide and 20 miles (30 km) long. They were unable to push past German forces and move deeper into France. On July 25, the Allies launched Operation Cobra, an attempt to break through the German lines and into the rest of France and Europe. Through bombings and a push by attacking US infantry divisions, gaps were created in the German forces. The US Third Army captured several key bridges, and the Allies were able to break through from Normandy into Brittany. By August 1, Allied forces began streaming into the interior of France.

On August 25, after four years of being occupied by the Germans, the Allies liberated Paris. On December 16, Hitler began a desperate attempt to push back the Allies from the Western Front. He ordered 250,000 of his troops to move across Belgium and Luxembourg in what would be the last large German offensive battle on this front: the Battle of the Bulge.[3] The combat raged until January 16, 1945, ending in the German army's defeat. The German troops retreated as they ran short on supplies and were overwhelmed by the Allies.

And the Red Army, fighting along the Eastern Front, had succeeded in pushing the German army back across Poland and Hungary. The Soviets forced the Germans to withdraw from Greece and southern Yugoslavia. By the end of 1944, the Germans still held half of Poland but were slowly being flanked by the Red Army pushing up through the Balkans.

By March 1945, the Allies had pushed across the Rhine River into Germany. The river was the last geographic barrier preventing the Allies from entering Germany. US, British, and French forces flooded into Germany and annihilated the Wehrmacht forces. On April 30, as Soviet troops entered central Berlin, Hitler shot himself in his bunker. Early on May 7, on behalf of all the Allied nations at war with Germany, Eisenhower accepted Germany's unconditional surrender in Reims, France. The next day, German commanders repeated their surrender to Soviet commanders in Berlin. Late on May 8, World War II officially ended.

INVISIBLE AIR FORCE

One key to the Allied success on D-day was the lack of the Luftwaffe. There was a German joke about the Luftwaffe not showing up that day: "If the plane in the sky was silver it was American, if it was blue it was British, if it was invisible it was ours."[4]

One type of Allied aircraft, the P-51 Mustang fighter, turned the tide of the air battle in the five months prior to D-day. The P-51 Mustang destroyed 4,950 German planes.[5] From May 1944 onward, the Luftwaffe was not a significant factor in the outcome of the war.

The Success of Many

D-day was a gamble. Bringing so many Allied troops across the channel from England and attacking the Germans on the beaches of Normandy could have gone horribly wrong and weakened the Allies' position rather than strengthen it. But the gamble paid off.

D-day was a success due in part to the incredible planning by the Allied commanders and staffs. But the Allied victory in France was mostly due to the bravery, leadership, and dedication of the men who carried out the massive invasion of Normandy. They piloted the

REMEMBERING THE SACRIFICES

There are several military cemeteries and memorials near the beaches of the Normandy invasion. The Normandy American Cemetery and Memorial in Colleville-sur-Mer, France, is considered US soil. It was built on the site of a temporary US cemetery established in 1944 and contains the bodies of 9,387 Americans killed on D-day or in subsequent battles.[6] It includes a colonnade, the Wall of the Missing, and a chapel. And the Caen-Normandy Memorial and Museum in Caen, France, tells the story of the Normandy invasion.

There are six cemeteries in the Normandy region for German soldiers. Many of the men were initially buried in scattered or isolated battle cemeteries and reburied in official cemeteries.

The United States has a D-day memorial in Bedford, Virginia, which lost 19 of its young men on D-day, the highest per capita loss of any US city.[7] The memorial includes a garden and a tableau of the invasion.

A sea of crosses marks graves at the Normandy American Cemetery and Memorial.

airplanes, crewed the ships, and landed on the beaches. Each one, playing his part, helped the Allies achieve victory. By the tens of thousands they pushed, many of the soldiers giving their lives for the cause of victory. And their sacrifice was not in vain. The success of the Normandy invasion changed the course of the war and history. This lone day was so significant it became and will forever be known by a single word: D-day.

TIMELINE

1933
Adolf Hitler becomes chancellor of Germany and creates a dictatorship.

1938
Hitler's Nazis invade and take over Austria.

1939
Germany invades Czechoslovakia and then Poland, the latter of which prompts the United Kingdom and other nations to declare war on Germany on September 3.

1940
The Nazis invade Denmark, Norway, France, Belgium, Luxembourg, and the Netherlands.

1941
The United States enters World War II following the bombing of Pearl Harbor in Hawaii on December 7.

1943
By the end of July, COSSAC creates a 113-page plan for Operation Overlord.

1943
In November, Franklin D. Roosevelt, Winston Churchill, and Joseph Stalin meet for the first time to discuss invasion plans and a push to defeat Hitler.

1943
In December, General Dwight D. Eisenhower becomes commander of Supreme Headquarters, Allied Expeditionary Forces.

1944
On February 12, Eisenhower receives orders to conduct Operation Overlord and land Allied troops in Europe.

1944
The Allies conduct Operations Fortitude North and South to mislead the Germans about the invasion site.

1944
On the night of June 5–6, Allied paratroopers and gliders begin invading Normandy, France.

TIMELINE

1944
At 5:50 a.m. on June 6, Allied bombers begin bombing German fortifications.

1944
On June 6, after the Allied battle fleet stopped firing at 6:20 a.m., Allied troops begin coming ashore at Normandy.

1944
By the end of June 6, Allied forces establish a foothold in Normandy.

1944
On July 25, the Allies begin Operation Cobra, the breakout from Normandy.

1944
The Allies liberate Paris, France, from German occupation on August 25.

1945
On January 16, the Allies defeat the Germans in the Battle of the Bulge.

1945
The Allies cross the Rhine River in March and push into Germany.

1945
On April 30, Hitler kills himself in Berlin, Germany.

1945
General Eisenhower accepts Germany's unconditional surrender on May 7.

1945
The war officially ends on May 8.

ESSENTIAL FACTS

Date of Event
June 6, 1944

Place of Event
Five beaches along the coastal area of France known as Normandy, directly across the English Channel from England, from the port of Cherbourg on the Cotentin Peninsula to the city of Caen.

Key Players
- Winston Churchill, prime minister of the United Kingdom

- Dwight D. Eisenhower, supreme commander of Allied Expeditionary Forces in Europe

- Adolf Hitler, chancellor of Germany and head of the Nazi Party

- Bernard Montgomery, commander of Allied ground forces

- Frederick E. Morgan, leader of COSSAC and a major planner of the D-day invasion

- Erwin Rommel, German commander

- Franklin D. Roosevelt, president of the United States

- Joseph Stalin, premier of the Soviet Union

Highlights of Event

- The United States actively joined World War II in December 1941, following Japan's attack on Pearl Harbor, Hawaii.

- COSSAC finished drafting a 113-page plan for Operation Overlord, the code name for the invasion of Normandy.

- General Dwight D. Eisenhower became commander of the Allied forces in Europe in 1943.

- Eisenhower received orders for Operation Overlord on February 12, 1944.

- Eisenhower gave the command for the invasion on June 5, but bad weather delayed the attack.

- On June 6, 1944, the Allies successfully landed 175,000 troops on the beaches of Normandy, launching the beginning of an attack that would end the war in Europe the following spring.

Quote

"This operation is not being planned with any alternatives. This operation is planned as a victory, and that's the way it's going to be. We're going down there, and we're throwing everything we have into it, and we're going to make it a success."—*General Dwight D. Eisenhower's words while preparing for the Allied invasion of Normandy, France, on June 6, 1944*

GLOSSARY

amphibious
A military operation that involves forces landing from the sea, or referring to equipment that is suitable for both land and water use.

armada
A big group of warships.

battery
A fortified position or location for a heavy gun.

breakwater
An offshore structure that protects the shore from waves.

bunker
A fortification that is mostly underground and has a concrete roof with openings for firing guns.

campaign
A military operation undertaken to achieve a large goal.

conscientious objector
Someone who refuses to serve in the military because of religious or moral beliefs.

demolition
The process of destroying something, especially with explosives.

emplacement
A position or location where a gun is located for firing.

fortification
A defensive wall or other kind of structure built to strengthen a place against an attack.

infantry
Soldiers who march or fight on foot.

intelligence
Collection of information that has military or political value.

lodgment area
A military base of operations formed from several troop landing sites.

morale
The mental or emotional condition of a person or group that is involved in a specific task.

offensive
A military campaign that attacks the enemy.

pillbox
A small, low building made of reinforced concrete that often contains machine guns or antitank guns.

reconnaissance
A military observation of a region in order to collect information about features or to locate the enemy.

theater
A specific geographic area where an armed conflict or war is taking place.

ADDITIONAL RESOURCES

Selected Bibliography

Ambrose, Stephen E. *D-Day: June 6, 1944: The Climactic Battle of World War II*. New York: Simon, 1994. Print.

Atkinson, Rick. *The Guns at Last Light: The War in Western Europe, 1944–1945*. New York: Holt, 2013. Print.

Beevor, Antony. *D-Day: The Battle for Normandy*. New York: Penguin, 2009. Print.

Further Readings

Levine, Joshua. *Operation Fortitude: The Greatest Hoax of the Second World War*. New York: Collins, 2012. Print.

Macintyre, Ben. *Double Cross: The True Story of the D-Day Spies*. New York: Crown, 2012. Print.

Vansant, Wayne. *Normandy: A Graphic History of D-Day, the Allied Invasion of Hitler's Fortress Europe*. Minneapolis: Zenith, 2012. Print.

Web Sites

To learn more about D-day, visit ABDO Publishing Company online at **www.abdopublishing.com**. Web sites about D-day are featured on our Book Links page. These links are routinely monitored and updated to provide the most current information available.

Places to Visit

National D-Day Memorial
PO Box 77
Bedford, VA 24523
800-351-3329
http://www.dday.org
This memorial, which includes a museum and exhibits, is located in the town that lost 19 soldiers in the D-day invasion.

National World War II Museum
945 Magazine Street
New Orleans, LA 70130
504-528-1944
http://www.nationalww2museum.org/index.html
This museum is dedicated to telling the story of the US experience during World War II, including D-Day.

Normandy American Cemetery and Memorial
Overlooking Omaha Beach, east of Saint Laurent-sur-Mer, Normandy, France
http://www.abmc.gov/cemeteries/cemeteries/no.php
The burial site of more than 9,000 US soldiers who died on D-day or in related battles, this cemetery is technically US soil and has memorials and commemorative exhibits.

SOURCE NOTES

Chapter 1. Taking a Gamble
1. "Holocaust Encyclopedia: D-Day." *USHMM.org*. United States Holocaust Memorial Museum, n.d. Web. 10 Oct. 2013.
2. "American Experience: D-Day Transcript." *PBS.org*. WGBH, 2009. Web. 10 Oct. 2013.
3. Stephen E. Ambrose. *D-Day: June 6, 1944: The Climactic Battle of World War II*. New York: Simon, 1994. Print. 277–278.
4. Ibid.
5. "The Archives of the D-Day Museum." *Ddaymuseum.co.uk*. Portsmouth City Council, 2012. Web. 10 Oct. 2013.
6. Victor Brooks. *The Normandy Campaign: From D-Day to the Liberation of Paris*. Cambridge, MA: Da Capo, 2002. 144. *Google Book Search*. Web. 10 Oct. 2013.

Chapter 2. Getting Involved
1. "Holocaust Encyclopedia: Introduction to the Holocaust." *USHMM.org*. United States Holocaust Memorial Museum, n.d. Web. 10 Oct. 2013.
2. Peter Grier, "Pearl Harbor Day: How Did Adolf Hitler React to the Attack?" *Christian Science Monitor*. Christian Science Monitor, 7 Dec. 2011. Web. 10 Oct. 2013.
3. "History of WW2: US Entry and Alliance." *History.co.uk*. AETN UK, 2013. Web. 10 Oct. 2013.
4. "On This Day: U.S. Declares War, Pacific Battle Widens." *New York Times*. New York Times, 2010. Web. 10 Oct. 2013.
5. Michael Ray. "Selective Service." *Britannica.com*. Encyclopaedia Britannica, 2013. Web. 10 Oct. 2013.
6. "Operation Torch." *History Learning Site*. HistoryLearningSite.co.uk, 2013. Web. 13 July 2013.
7. "WWII Behind Closed Doors: Stalin, the Nazis, and the West." *PBS.org*. Public Broadcasting Service, 2013. Web. 10 Oct. 2013.

Chapter 3. Planning and Preparing
1. Owen Platt. *Bodyguard: The Secret Plan That Saved D-Day*. Lincoln, NE: iUniverse, 2004. 37. *Google Book Search*. Web. 10 Oct. 2013.
2. "History, Chief of Staff to Supreme Allied Command." *History.army.mil*. US Army Center of Military History, 27 Sept. 2013. Web. 13 July 2013.
3. "The War: D-Day (June 6, 1944). *PBS.org*. WETA, 2007. Web. 10 Oct. 2013.
4. Ibid.
5. Stephen E. Ambrose. *D-Day: June 6, 1944: The Climactic Battle of World War II*. New York: Simon, 1994. Print. 85.
6. "Operational Unit Diagrams." *Army.mil*. US Army, n.d. Web. 10 Oct. 2013.
7. "The War: D-Day (June 6, 1944)." *PBS.org*. WETA, 2007. Web. 10 Oct. 2013.

8. Stephen E. Ambrose. *D-Day: June 6, 1944: The Climactic Battle of World War II.* New York: Simon, 1994. Print. 107

9. "The War: D-Day (June 6, 1944). *PBS.org*. WETA, 2007. Web. 10 Oct. 2013.

10. Ibid.

11. Antony Beevor. *D-Day: The Battle for Normandy*. New York: Penguin Books, 2009. Print. 45.

12. Jeremy Gypton. "Along the Atlantic Wall: Rommel's Last Battle." *Militaryhistoryonline.com*. Jeremy Gypton, 2002. Web. 10 Oct. 2013.

Chapter 4. Deceiving the Enemy

1. Henrik O. Lunde. *Hitler's Pre-Emptive War: The Battle for Norway, 1940*. Drexel Hill, PA: Casemate, 2009. 15. *Google Book Search*. Web. 21 Oct. 2013.

2. Anthony Cave Brown. *Bodyguard: The Extraordinary True Story Behind D-Day*. Guilford, CT: Lyons Press, 2002. 472. *Google Book Search*. Web. 21 Oct. 2013.

3. Stephen E. Ambrose. *D-Day: June 6, 1944: The Climactic Battle of World War II.* New York: Simon, 1994. Print. 83.

4. Ibid.

Chapter 5. Gearing Up

1. "The Higgins Boat." *Stanford University*. Stanford University, n.d. Web. 10 Oct. 2013.

2. Ibid.

3. "Operational Unit Diagrams." *Army.mil*. US Army, n.d. Web. 10 Oct. 2013.

4. Center of Military History. *Omaha Beachhead (6 June–13 June 1944)*. Washington, DC: US Army, 1994. 13. *Google Book Search*. Web. 10 Oct. 2013.

5. "The Higgins Boat." *Stanford University*. Stanford University, n.d. Web. 10 Oct. 2013.

6. Ibid.

7. Charles B. MacDonald. "Slapton Sands: The Cover-Up That Never Was." *Navy Department Library*. US Navy, n.d. Web. 10 Oct. 2013.

8. Stephen E. Ambrose. *D-Day: June 6, 1944: The Climactic Battle of World War II.* New York: Simon, 1994. Print. 54–56.

9. Ibid. 31–32.

10. "Secret Pipeline of WWII." *Aoghs.org*. American Oil & Gas Historical Society, 2012. Web. 11 Oct. 2013.

11. Stephen E. Ambrose. *D-Day: June 6, 1944: The Climactic Battle of World War II.* New York: Simon, 1994. Print. 152.

12. Ibid. 154.

13. Ibid. 151–152.

SOURCE NOTES CONTINUED

Chapter 6. Loading and Launching

1. Stephen E. Ambrose. *D-Day: June 6, 1944: The Climactic Battle of World War II.* New York: Simon, 1994. Print. 170.

2. Ibid.

3. "Transcript of General Dwight D. Eisenhower's Order of the Day (1944)." *ourdocuments.gov*. National History Day, National Archives and Records Administration, USA Freedom Corps, n.d. Web. 15 July 2013.

4. Dwight D. Eisenhower. "D-Day, 1944." *Archives.gov*. National Archives and Records Administration, n.d. Web. 10 Oct. 2013.

5. "D-Day Airborne and Beach Assault." *Army.mil*. US Army, n.d. Web. 20 Oct. 2013.

6. "The CG-4A Glider." *Exploringthenorth.com*. Vivian Wood, 2002. Web. 10 Oct. 2013.

7. Stephen E. Ambrose. *D-Day: June 6, 1944: The Climactic Battle of World War II.* New York: Simon, 1994. Print. 174.

8. "506th Parachute Infantry Regiment, 101st Airborne Division." *Military.com*. Military Advantage, 2013. Web. 10 Oct. 2013.

9. Stephen E. Ambrose. *D-Day: June 6, 1944: The Climactic Battle of World War II.* New York: Simon, 1994. Print. 211.

10. Ibid. 239.

11. Ibid.

12. Ibid. 221.

Chapter 7. Going Ashore

1. Stephen E. Ambrose. *D-Day: June 6, 1944: The Climactic Battle of World War II.* New York: Simon, 1994. Print. 57.

2. Ibid. 262–263.

3. Ibid. 274.

4. Ibid. 256.

5. Ibid. 271.

6. Ibid. 275.

Chapter 8. Beach by Beach

1. Stephen E. Ambrose. *D-Day: June 6, 1944: The Climactic Battle of World War II.* New York: Simon, 1994. Print. 279.

2. Jeremy C. Schwendiman. *Saving Lives, Saving Honor: The 39th Evacuation Hospital during World War II.* Jeremy C. Schwendiman, 2008. 118. *Google Book Search*. Web. 10 Oct. 2013.

3. "D-Day: June 6, 1944." *Nationalww2musuem.org*. National WWII Museum, New Orleans, n.d. Web. 10 Oct. 2013.

4. Ibid.

5. Ibid.

6. Ibid.

7. Stephen E. Ambrose. *D-Day: June 6, 1944: The Climactic Battle of World War II.* New York: Simon, 1994. Print. 329–330.

8. "D-Day: June 6, 1944." *Nationalww2musuem.org*. National WWII Museum, New Orleans, n.d. Web. 10 Oct. 2013.

9. "Chapter VII: Introduction to Battle." *History.army.mil.com*. US Army Center of Military History, 27 June 2011. Web. 10 Oct. 2013.

10. "D-Day: June 6, 1944." *Nationalww2musuem.org*. National WWII Museum, New Orleans, n.d. Web. 10 Oct. 2013.

11. "Miracle Harbor." *The Navy Department Library*. US Navy, n.d. Web. 10 Oct. 2013.

12. "D-Day: June 6, 1944." *Nationalww2musuem.org*. National WWII Museum, New Orleans, n.d. Web. 10 Oct. 2013.

13. Ibid.

14. D-Day Museum. "D-Day and the Battle of Normandy: Your Questions Answered." *Ddaymuseum.co.uk*. Portsmouth City Council, 2012. Web. 10 Oct. 2013.

15. Ibid.

Chapter 9. The Next Day and Beyond

1. D-Day Museum. "D-Day and the Battle of Normandy: Your Questions Answered." *Ddaymuseum.co.uk*. Portsmouth City Council, 2012. Web. 10 Oct. 2013.

2. "D-Day: June 6, 1944." *Nationalww2musuem.org*. National WWII Museum, New Orleans, n.d. Web. 10 Oct. 2013.

3. "Dec. 16, 1944: Battle of the Bulge." *History.com*. A&E Television Networks, 2013. Web. 10 Oct. 2013.

4. Stephen E. Ambrose. *D-Day: June 6, 1944: The Climactic Battle of World War II.* New York: Simon, 1994. Print. 578.

5. "The P51 Mustang." *History Learning Site*. HistoryLearningSite.co.uk, 2013. Web. 10 Oct. 2013.

6. "Normandy American Cemetery and Memorial. *Abmc.gov*. American Battle Monuments Commission, n.d. Web. 10 Oct. 2013.

7. Boyd Childress. "National D-Day Memorial." *Encyclopedia Virginia*. Virginia Foundation for the Humanities, 23 Nov. 2010. Web. 10 Oct. 2013.

INDEX

Army Rangers, 83–84
Atlantic Wall, 41–42, 75

beach jumpers, 46
beach obstacles, 9–10, 32, 40–41, 54, 76, 77, 80, 81–82, 84–85
Bradley, Omar, 83
Bulge, Battle of the, 92

cemeteries and memorials, 94
Cherbourg, France, 31, 32, 34–35, 65, 66, 91
choosing Normandy, 32–33
Churchill, Winston, 23, 25, 31, 48
code breakers, 44
Combined Chiefs of Staff to the Supreme Allied Commander, 30–31, 32, 33
Cotentin Peninsula, 35, 67, 91

D-day meaning, 12
double agents, 47
draft, US, 24

Eastern Front, 89, 92
Eastridge, Ralph, 61
Eisenhower, Dwight D., 26–27, 33, 37, 45–46, 48, 52, 62–63, 93
English Channel, 7, 29, 32, 33, 46, 48, 51, 56, 61, 65, 67, 71, 74, 85, 91, 94

First US Army Group, 45–46
Fitzgerald, John, 68
French Resistance, 38–40

gliders, 31, 40, 64, 65, 68, 71
Gockel, Franz, 74
Gold Beach, 8–9, 35, 81, 84–85

Higgins, Andrew, 51–53
Higgins boats, 9, 51–53, 74–75, 79, 80
Hitler, Adolf, 7, 11, 12, 16, 17–19, 21, 26, 27, 30, 31, 40, 44–45, 46, 48, 56, 84, 87, 89, 92, 93
Holocaust, 18

Juno Beach, 8–9, 35, 85–86

Keitel, Wilhelm, 11

landing craft, tank, 53, 74
landing craft, vehicle and personnel, 51–53, 72
landing ship, tank, 53, 58, 61
Luftwaffe, 8, 68, 93

MacArthur, Douglas, 20
Mace, M. Andre, 67
Marshall, George C., 21, 40
mines and minesweepers, 9, 54, 56, 71, 74, 75, 77, 82, 85, 86
Montgomery, Bernard, 22, 33
Morgan, Frederick, 26, 30, 33
Mulberry harbor, 57, 85

Nimitz, Chester, 20

"old ladies," 72
Omaha Beach, 8–9, 10, 35, 67, 72–73, 74, 75, 81–84, 85, 91
Operation Bodyguard, 35–36, 43, 48
Operation Bolero, 35, 37
Operation Fortitude North, 43, 44–45, 47–48
Operation Fortitude South, 43, 45–48
Operation Neptune, 36
Operation Overlord, 11, 30–37, 41, 43, 44, 51, 56, 57, 62, 79, 89
Operation Titanic, 65
Operation Torch, 21–25

paratroopers, 8, 63–66, 68
Pas de Calais, France, 31, 32, 33, 45, 46
Patton, George S., Jr., 45–46
Pearl Harbor, Hawaii, 18, 72
Pike, Malvin, 9–10
Pipeline Under the Ocean (PLUTO), 56–57
planning, 12, 26–27, 29–33, 41, 48, 94
preparing the troops, 57–59

Roach, George, 82–83
Rommel, Erwin, 22, 40, 45
Roosevelt, Franklin D., 18, 20, 23, 25–26

Sainte Mère Église, France, 65, 67, 81
Sears, Alfred, 10
Slapton Sands, 53
Sommers, Martin, 72
specialized tanks, 54–55
Stalin, Joseph, 25, 89
Supreme Headquarters, Allied Expeditionary Forces, 33
Sword Beach, 8–9, 35, 85, 86–87

Tegtmeyer, Charles, 82

Utah Beach, 8–10, 35, 53, 67, 71, 74, 79–81, 83

Versailles, Treaty of, 15, 16, 17
Vichy government, 22–23

Wehrmacht, 12, 21, 22, 93
Weimar Republic, 16
Western Front, 30, 92
Wilson, Woodrow, 15
World War I, 8, 12, 15, 16, 17, 18, 23, 24
World War II, 7, 8, 12, 19, 23, 24, 27, 54, 64, 93

ABOUT THE AUTHOR

Marcia Amidon Lusted has written more than 80 books and 400 magazine articles for young readers. She is also an editor, a writing instructor, and a musician. She lives in New Hampshire.

ABOUT THE CONSULTANT

Dr. Peter R. Mansoor, colonel, US Army (retired), is the General Raymond E. Mason Jr. Chair of Military History at Ohio State University. His 26-year military career included two combat tours in Iraq. He is the author of *The GI Offensive in Europe: The Triumph of American Infantry Divisions, 1941–1945*, which was the winner of the 2000 Society for Military History Distinguished Book Award, as well as two books on the Iraq War.